COMMON CORE
STANDARDS

for | Elementary
Grades K–2 Math
& English Language Arts

Edited by *John Kendall*

COMMON CORE
STANDARDS

for | Elementary
Grades K–2 Math
& English Language Arts

Amber Evenson

Monette McIver

Susan Ryan

Amitra Schwols

ASCD

Alexandria, Virginia USA

McREL

Mid-continent Research for Education and Learning
Denver, Colorado USA

1703 N. Beauregard St. • Alexandria, VA 22311-1714 USA
Phone: 800-933-2723 or 703-578-9600 • Fax: 703-575-5400
Website: www.ascd.org • E-mail: member@ascd.org
Author guidelines: www.ascd.org/write

M⋅REL

Mid-continent Research for Education and Learning
4601 DTC Boulevard, Suite 500
Denver, CO 80237 USA
Phone: 303-337-0990 • Fax: 303-337-3005
Website: www.mcrel.org • E-mail: info@mcrel.org

PAPERBACK ISBN: 978-1-4166-1465-4   ASCD product #113014   n5/13

Also available as an e-book (see Books in Print for the ISBNs).

Quantity discounts: 10–49 copies, 10%; 50+ copies, 15%; for 1,000 or more copies, call 800-933-2723, ext. 5634, or 703-575-5634. For desk copies: www.ascd.org/deskcopy

Library of Congress Cataloging-in-Publication Data
Evenson, Amber.
   Common core standards for elementary grades K-2 math & English language arts a quick-start guide / Amber Evenson, Monette McIver, Susan Ryan, Amitra Schwols ; edited by John Kendall.
      pages cm
   Includes bibliographical references.
   ISBN 978-1-4166-1465-4 (pbk. : alk. paper)   1. Mathematics—Study and teaching (Elemen-tary)—United States.   2. Mathematics—Study and teaching (Elementary)—Standards—United States.   3. Language arts (Elementary)—Curricula—United States—States.   4. Language arts (Elementary)—Standards—United States—States. I. Title.
   QA135.6.E848 2013
   372.602'1873—dc23
                                                                          2013006299

22 21 20 19 18 17 16 15 14 13   1 2 3 4 5 6 7 8 9 10 11 12

COMMON CORE STANDARDS

for | Elementary
Grades K–2 Math
& English Language Arts

Editor's Preface

This book is part of a series on the Common Core State Standards designed to help educators quickly acquire a deeper understanding of what the standards mean, how they are related within and across grades, and how they help to ensure that, at the end of their schooling, students are prepared to succeed in postsecondary education or the working world.

To help facilitate that understanding, the authors of this guide provide a narrative "unpacking" of the standards. An *unpacking* is a close analysis of the language and structure of standards designed to make the content of the standards clear. The narrative approach to unpacking you will find here allows the authors to convey the many connections that can be found in the standards, and it seems a wiser approach than the kind of unpacking that breaks standards statements into disconnected pieces of knowledge and skill. To maintain coherence, the authors follow the structure of the standards closely; however, even a cursory comparison of the Common Core standards for English language arts and literacy (ELA/literacy) and the Common Core standards for mathematics makes obvious the striking structural differences between the two. That's why you will notice a very different approach to the discussion in the two subject-area sections of this guide.

Within the introduction to each subject area, the authors provide an overview of the standards and the structure they will use to organize the discussion to come. In the ELA/literacy standards, individual grade-level standards serve to advance what is called an *anchor standard*, which describes an overall goal and area of focus. Such a design invites a close comparison of standards at adjacent grades to clarify how each standard builds from grade to grade and within each grade. It's a logical approach given that language arts and literacy processes, such as reading and writing, grow more complex over the years—in part because of the increasing complexity of the reading material on which many of the standards depend.

The Common Core's approach to mathematics does not include anchor standards, and the mathematics standards have a more complex structure. Whereas the ELA/literacy standards feature the same topics at nearly every grade, the math standards do not. It's probable that this organization reflects a deliberate intent to avoid a common pitfall observed in prior state standards for mathematics, which is the tendency to revisit the same content over again each year. Mathematics concepts and skills are more discrete than the kinds of processes students use in ELA classes, and, once mastered, these concepts and skills reappear principally as either subskills or fundamental concepts required in service of more complex skills and tasks. As a result, new mathematics topics appear or disappear with each grade, requiring the authors of this guide to provide, in their Part II treatment of mathematics standards, a more expansive cross-standard description of the connections that apply.

Part III of the guide addresses lesson planning and lessons. It includes three sample lessons for each subject area, built to reflect the best of what we know about designing instruction. As the starting point for these lessons, the authors selected standards that, in light of previous state standards, teachers are likely to find instructionally challenging. The sample lessons also serve to show how the new standards, while they may present a greater challenge to students, are also articulated through the grades to ensure that students will come to each grade knowing what they need to in order to master the new and rigorous content.

John Kendall

Acknowledgments

We would like to acknowledge Kirsten Miller and John Kendall for their crucial role in making our thoughts much more readable; Greg Gallagher and the North Dakota Curriculum Initiative committee, who provided us with valuable insights into the challenges facing teachers as they begin to work with the Common Core standards; Ceri Dean for her step-by-step guide to lesson planning; Jan Killick, Barbara Browning, and Kathleen Dempsey for their collaboration and content expertise in developing the lessons; Carrie Germeroth, who provided insight and information from an early childhood education perspective; and our families, for supporting us as we worked on this project.

Introduction

In July 2009, nearly all state school superintendents and the nation's governors joined in an effort to identify a common set of standards in mathematics and English language arts, with the goal of providing a clear, shared set of expectations that would prepare students for success in both college and career. The Common Core State Standards Initiative (CCSSI) brought together researchers, academics, teachers, and others who routed multiple drafts of the standards to representatives including curriculum directors, content specialists, and technical advisors from all participating state departments of education. By spring 2010, drafts were submitted for comment to the national subject-area organizations and posted for public comment. In June 2010, the final versions were posted to a dedicated website: www.corestandards.org. (A minor update of the standards was posted in October 2010.)

At press time, 45 states, as well as Washington, D.C., and two territories, have adopted the Common Core State Standards (CCSS) for mathematics. (Minnesota has adopted the ELA/literacy standards but not the mathematics standards. Texas, Alaska, Virginia, and Nebraska have indicated that they do not plan to adopt either set, although both Virginia and Nebraska have aligned the Common Core standards with their existing standards, and Alaska has adopted a new set of standards that reflect the Common Core.)

Adoption of the standards is, of course, voluntary for states and does not include a commitment to any other programs or policies. However, states that have adopted these standards will be eligible to join one of two federally funded assessment consortia that are currently tasked with developing assessments for the Common Core—the Smarter Balanced Assessment Consortium (SBAC) or the Partnership for Assessment of Readiness for College and Careers (PARCC). PARCC has indicated that it will be delivering assessments for grades K–12. Its assessments for K–2 will be formative, while those for grades 3–12 will include both summative and nonsummative assessment components. SBAC has indicated that it will be creating assessments for grades 3–8 and 11 only. Sharing assessments across states promises financial relief from notoriously expensive state assessments. In addition, federal programs such as Race to the Top have required that applicants demonstrate that they have joined with other states in adopting a common set of standards and an assessment program. Although states may form new consortia, many either have opted to join or are considering joining SBAC or PARCC.

Sharing a set of standards across states offers other advantages. For example, teachers' well-designed lesson plans targeting Common Core standards will be immediately useful to a large number of colleagues. The shared language of standards should also provide teachers with more opportunities to participate in very specific discussions about content, a process that has been hampered somewhat by the variety of ways states have described virtually the same content.

For a lengthier discussion of the Common Core standards, including their link to previous standards-based education efforts and the benefits and challenges the Common Core presents, see *Understanding Common Core State Standards* (Kendall, 2011), the first booklet in this series. We also encourage readers to explore numerous resources available online at corestandards.org, especially the standards documents themselves (CCSSI, 2010c, 2010g) and the guidelines for adapting standards instruction for English language learners (CCSSI, 2010a) and students with disabilities (CCSSI, 2010b).

About This Guide

This guide is part of a series intended to further the discussion and understanding of Common Core standards on a subject-specific and grade-level basis and to provide immediate guidance to teachers who must either adapt existing lessons and activities to incorporate the Common Core or develop new lessons to teach concepts not addressed in their previous state standards.

In the pages ahead, we will look at the general structure of the Common Core standards for both ELA/literacy and mathematics in the lower elementary grades (K–2). In Part I, we focus on ELA/literacy, exploring the links among the standards' four strands and looking closely at the three domains within the Reading strand. In Part II, we examine the content in and connections among the mathematics domains, highlighting the mathematical practice standards with the strongest connections to each mathematics domain. In Part III, we turn to practical lesson planning with the Common Core, presenting a process for creating standards-based lessons that make the best use of the effective instructional strategies explored in *Classroom Instruction That Works, 2nd edition* (Dean, Hubbell, Pitler, & Stone, 2012). The guide concludes with an illustration of this process's outcome: six sample lessons that address Common Core standards identified as representing notable changes to the current practices of teachers working in the primary grade levels.

PART I

English Language Arts and Literacy

CHAPTER 1

About the Common Core ELA/Literacy Standards for Grades K–2

This chapter focuses on key areas of the Common Core State Standards for English Language Arts and Literacy that represent the most significant changes to commonly used curricula and presents an overview of how the standards are organized, fit together, and reinforce one another. Reviewing the essential student knowledge and skills in the Common Core will allow teachers to quickly understand how they might adjust the materials and strategies used in their classroom to best meet these new expectations.

Focus Areas and Instructional Implications

Although the Common Core ELA/literacy standards are comprehensive and address a broad range of communication skills, in grades K–2, they place particular emphasis on three key areas: foundational skills for early reading, building disciplinary knowledge through complex informational texts, and writing and speaking about texts. Let's take a closer look at each area and consider its implications for teachers.

Foundational skills for early reading

The Common Core provides detailed guidance on the specific early reading knowledge and skills that children should attain when learning to decode texts and build reading fluency. Much of this knowledge and many of these skills, such as print concepts, phonological awareness, and phonetic knowledge, have also been recommended in key reports by the National Reading Panel (National Institute of Child Health and Human Development, 2000). The standards call for foundational reading skills to be central to curriculum and instruction and to be systematically integrated into a wide spectrum of student language activities (Coleman & Pimental, 2012). The foundational skills standards do not represent a significant change from former state standards or common early reading curricula. However, teachers of young children will note that these standards provide very specific guidance in the skills that students need to acquire in order to read proficiently by 3rd grade, and so some curricular and instructional adjustments may be required.

Building knowledge through complex informational text

During the last decade, the amount of nonfiction included in reading textbooks and on national reading tests such as the National Assessment of Educational Progress has been increasing (National Assessment Governing Board, 2010). The Common Core adds momentum to this trend, calling for a balance between literature and informational texts in the curriculum.

Considering that as little as 7 percent of current elementary school instructional reading is expository (CCSSI, 2010d), adoption of the Common Core means elementary teachers will need to increase the number of informational texts they ask their students to read. Rather than compete with literary reading for "ELA class time," this reading should support learning across the curriculum, helping to build literacy and content-area knowledge in science, social studies, the arts, and other subjects. Additionally, it's essential that students' reading abilities not limit their acquisition of knowledge in areas like history and science; instruction should be designed to allow students to listen to complex informational texts that they may not be able to read on their own yet. This focus on using literacy skills to support subject-area learning is found throughout the Common Core standards, which also emphasize subject-specific vocabulary and writing about informational texts.

Writing and speaking about texts

The Common Core standards emphasize writing and speaking in response to stories and informational texts, including the comparison of ideas in texts on the same topic or theme. Students write pieces in which they support an opinion about a text and pieces in which they explain information from a text. In both cases, students provide supporting details in their writing and speaking that are drawn directly from the material they read and that has been read to them.

Teachers may support students' reading and writing about texts by increasing the number of text-based questions that they ask (Coleman & Pimentel, 2012). *Text-based questions* are those that can be answered only by referring to details in the text. Currently, many questions in the curriculum are designed to develop background knowledge or to help students make connections between the text and their personal experiences. These types of questions will remain important during prereading exercises and as support strategies, but Appendix A to the ELA/literacy standards document recommends that the bulk of questions teachers use during instruction be answerable only by examining the text. Additionally, the writers of the Common Core advise teachers to favor graphic organizers and activities that ask students to provide specific quotations from the text as evidence. As teachers begin to implement the Common Core standards, they should inventory and review their current curriculum to identify and modify the types of questions they typically use. Teachers who implement the Common Core standards will likely also need to increase the number of student writing activities based on texts that students read or listen to, decreasing their use of writing activities in which students respond to a prompt that draws only on prior knowledge or experiences.

How the Standards Are Organized

The Common Core English language arts and literacy standards present content within a highly organized structure. Content is organized first by strands and then grouped under more specific headings. The standards themselves provide the most detailed level of content description: statements of student knowledge and skills for particular grades. In elementary school, there are ELA/literacy standards for each grade, K–5. In addition, each grade-level set of content standards (with the exception of a subset of the reading standards; see p. 35) can be traced back to the set of College and Career Readiness Anchor (CCRA) standards that broadly describe what students should know and be able to do by the time they graduate high school.

To further clarify the structure of the Common Core standards, we will look at each organizational component in turn.

Strands

The ELA/literacy standards are sorted into four strands: Reading, Writing, Speaking and Listening, and Language. The first three of these categories will be familiar, as they have been used to organize content in numerous state ELA standards documents. The category of Language, however, was found less frequently in state standards. The Common Core Language strand describes knowledge and skills that cross all the strands. Grammar, for example, is applicable to both writing and speaking activities, and vocabulary is an important element of reading, writing, speaking, and listening. The strands in the Common Core are also distinguished from some state standards in that research skills and media literacy are not separate categories; research is addressed in the Common Core Writing strand, and media is embedded throughout all strands, although it is most emphasized in the Speaking and Listening strand.

The Reading strand is further divided into three subsections, known as domains: Reading Literature, Reading Informational Text, and Reading

Foundational Skills. The standards in the first two domains are parallel, addressing the same basic reading skills but describing them in ways specific to reading fiction versus reading nonfiction. The Foundational Skills domain addresses content related to early reading, including phonemic awareness, decoding, and fluency. In this guide, we examine the similar Reading Literature and Reading Informational Text domains together in Chapter 2 and devote Chapter 3 to Reading Foundational Skills.

Each strand has an associated abbreviation code to identify its particular numbered standards, with each of the three domains of the Reading strand receiving its own shorthand:

- Reading Literature (RL)
- Reading Informational Text (RI)
- Reading Foundational Skills (RF)
- Writing (W)
- Speaking and Listening (SL)
- Language (L)

These strand abbreviations are used as part of the CCSSI's official identification system, which provides a unique identifier for each standard in the Common Core and can be very useful to school staffs developing crosswalks, planning lessons, and sharing lesson plans. For example, the fifth standard in the Writing strand can be referred to as "Writing Standard 5" or, using the full, formal "dot notation," as "CCSS.ELA-Literacy.W.5." To speak specifically of a standard for a particular grade, the grade designation is inserted between the strand and standard number: "CCSS.ELA-Literacy.W.1.5," for example, is Writing Standard 5 for 1st grade. In this guide, we use an abbreviated form of this identification system, dropping the common prefix and using only the strand and standard number (e.g., W.5) in our general discussion. We have included the grade-level indicators in figures that present or refer to standards at various grade levels and in the sample lessons.

Headings

Within each strand, a set of two or more topic headings provides further organization. The same headings span all grade levels. In the Language strand, for example, the standards are organized under three headings: Conventions of Standard English, Knowledge of Language, and Vocabulary Acquisition and Use. The headings provide users with an overview of the topics that the particular strands address, group standards that share a similar focus, and provide context for understanding individual standards. For example, the Craft and Structure heading within the Reading strand signals that the standards beneath it will focus on the various choices that authors make when developing (crafting) and organizing (structuring) their writing.

College and Career Readiness Anchor standards

As noted, the College and Career Readiness Anchor standards define the knowledge and skills students should acquire in each content strand over the course of their K–12 education. The more specific, grade-level content standard statements spell out the aspects of CCRA knowledge and skills appropriate for students within that grade. In other words, there is a version of every anchor standard for each grade level, and every grade level has the same anchor standards. For illustration, see Figure 1.1, which displays the kindergarten, 1st grade, and 2nd grade versions of the same anchor standard within the Reading strand's Reading Literature domain. Note that in contrast to the rest of the Common Core standards for ELA/ literacy, standards within the Reading strand's Foundational Skills domain are not directly associated with anchor standards.

The use of anchor standards provides overarching goals for student learning. When a single content standard includes many details and various aspects, teachers can identify that standard's primary focus by referring to its associated anchor standard. The progression of grade-level standards provides a structure that indicates how students' skills are expected to advance over time. As teachers assess their students, the continuum of grade-level standards in the Common Core may enhance their understanding of how specific skills develop. Additional resources have also been developed to help teachers understand the precursor and post-cursor skills for the Common Core standards at specific grade levels. The National Center for the Improvement of Educational Assessment has identified research-based learning progressions for use with the Common Core (Hess, 2011), and the Center on Instruction at RMC Research Corporation has identified learning progressions for the standards within the Reading Foundational Skills domain (Kosanovich & Verhagen, 2012).

Figure 1.1 | **Lower Elementary Grade-Specific Versions of a CCRA Standard**

CCRA	Kindergarten	Grade 1	Grade 2
RL.3 Analyze how and why individuals, events, and ideas develop and interact over the course of a text.	**RL.K.3** With prompting and support, identify characters, settings, and major events in a story.	**RL.1.3** Describe characters, settings, and major events in a story, using key details.	**RL.2.3** Describe how characters in a story respond to major events and challenges.

Connections Across Content Areas

It is important to note that although standards for literacy in history/social studies, science, and technical subjects are described separately in the Common Core standards for grades 6–12, they are fully integrated into the standards for grades K–5. The standards for reading, writing, speaking and listening, and language should be applied across the curriculum in elementary classrooms. For example, students will be expected to use skills articulated in the reading standards when reading history texts, and skills addressed in writing and speaking and listening standards when reporting the results of science experiments. In this way, the Common Core ELA/literacy standards work in conjunction with other subject-area standards and provide a foundation for a broad spectrum of student learning.

Appendices to the ELA/Literacy Standards

In addition to the standards themselves, the Common Core standards document for ELA/literacy includes a set of three appendices that provide further clarification and support.

Appendix A (CCSSI, 2010d) explains the research base and rationale for many of the key aspects of the standards. It describes how to use the Common Core text complexity model, which includes three factors for determining the appropriate complexity of texts for each grade range, beginning with grades 2–3. Appendix A also describes the three major text types required by the writing standards: opinion, informational, and narration. The role of oral language in literacy is also described in this appendix, as are various aspects of the Language strand, including phonemes, graphemes, syllabification, and vocabulary.

Appendix B (CCSSI, 2010e) supports teachers' efforts to determine appropriate levels of text complexity by excerpting portions of particular texts that illustrate the level of complexity required of students within each grade band. The Common Core standards for elementary school include two text complexity bands, grades 2–3 and grades 4–5, but Appendix B also includes exemplar texts for independent and group reading activities appropriate for grades K–1. Short performance tasks accompany the exemplar texts and indicate the types of activities and student performances that support specific reading standards.

The standards document's Appendix C (CCSSI, 2010f) provides annotated samples of student writing for each grade level that meet or exceed the minimum level of proficiency the standards demand. Examples are provided across all three of the text types: opinion, informational, and narrative writing. In most cases, the samples are accompanied by a description of the context for writing (prompt, requirements, audience, and purpose). Annotations clarify how the sample meets the requirements of the grade-level standards.

* * *

As noted, our intention in Part I of this guide is to provide a sense of the meaning of each ELA/literacy standard for the primary grades (K–2) and explain how the standards are related to each other across both grade levels and strands. Readers should be aware that what we present are examples of such connections; we do not mean to suggest that no other connections can or should be made. Teachers should build on the information here to strengthen their own practice and enhance their implementation of the Common Core standards.

Now that we've reviewed the overall structure of the Common Core ELA/literacy standards, let's examine each strand in greater depth.

CHAPTER 2

Reading Literature and Reading Informational Text

The Common Core's reading standards address both learning how to read and reading comprehension. The basic early reading skills that build students' ability to decode words are found in the standards of the Reading Foundational Skills (RF) domain, which extends only through grade 5. Reading Foundational Skills is the focus of Chapter 3. In this chapter, we will explore the reading comprehension skills found in the other two domains of the Reading strand, which extend all the way through grade 12: the Standards for Reading Literature ("Reading Literature" or "RL") and the Standards for Reading Informational Text ("Reading Informational Text" or "RI").

In the primary grades, these two domains provide the basis for later learning by introducing children to a variety of text types, including both fiction and informational texts. Because students in grades K–2 are just learning to read, it's recommended that teachers use read-alouds or other group reading and listening activities to expose these students to a range of rich, engaging books that will support their learning across the content areas. Teachers can foster this learning by asking students to respond to the details in books, retelling stories or information, and expressing opinions about what they have heard and read.

The Reading Literature and Reading Informational Text domains have an identical structure, and the standards in each domain are similar, although they highlight key differences between reading fiction and nonfiction. Both the Reading Literature and Reading Informational Text domains share the same 10 CCRA standards, as explained in Chapter 1. The anchor standards describe what students should know and be able to do by the time they graduate from high school. Each standard in kindergarten, 1st grade, and 2nd grade has a corresponding CCRA standard, which describes the standard's overall goal across grades in preparing students for the demands of college or career. In other words, each Reading Literature standard has a parallel standard in Reading Informational Text, both of which are tied to the same CCRA standard. The Reading Literature and Reading Informational Text domains also organize standards under the same four headings: Key Ideas and Details, Craft and Structure, Integration of Knowledge and Ideas, and Range of Reading and Level of Text Complexity.

Figure 2.1 provides an overview of the Reading Literature and Reading Informational Text domains at the lower elementary level.

Our discussion of the reading comprehension standards will alternate between literature and informational text. We'll move from one topic heading to the next, using excerpts from the Common Core to frame the discussion.

Key Ideas and Details

The Key Ideas and Details heading covers standards that address students' ability to retell the main ideas and details of a text. For literature, this means recalling the basic events, people, and places in stories. Figure 2.2 shows the sequence of the Key Ideas and Details standards within the Reading Literature domain. Differences in phrasing from the prior grade level are in boldface to highlight how the standards' content changes from grade to grade.

Reading Standard 1 is identical in the literature and informational text domains, where it is abbreviated as RL.1 and RI.1, respectively. This

Figure 2.1 | **The Reading Literature and Reading Informational Text Domains: Grades K–2 Overview**

Heading	CCRA Standard	Kindergarten Standards	Grade 1 Standards	Grade 2 Standards
Key Ideas and Details	R.1	RL.K.1 RI.K.1	RL.1.1 RI.1.1	RL.2.1 RI.2.1
	R.2	RL.K.2 RI.K.2	RL.1.2 RI.1.2	RL.2.2 RI.2.2
	R.3	RL.K.3 RI.K.3	RL.1.3 RI.1.3	RL.2.3 RI.2.3
Craft and Structure	R.4	RL.K.4 RI.K.4	RL.1.4 RI.1.4	RL.2.4 RI.2.4
	R.5	RL.K.5 RI.K.5	RL.1.5 RI.1.5	RL.2.5 RI.2.5
	R.6	RL.K.6 RI.K.6	RL.1.6 RI.1.6	RL.2.6 RI.2.6
Integration of Knowledge and Ideas	R.7	RL.K.7 RI.K.7	RL.1.7 RI.1.7	RL.2.7 RI.2.7
	R.8	RI.K.8	RI.1.8	RI.2.8
	R.9	RL.K.9 RI.K.9	RL.1.9 RI.1.9	RL.2.9 RI.2.9
Range of Reading and Level of Text Complexity	R.10	RL.K.10 RI.K.10	RL.1.10 RI.1.10	RL.2.10 RI.2.10

standard requires students to ask and answer questions about books that they read or that are read to them. Students support their answers to questions by referring to key details in the story. At all grade levels, Reading Standard 1 works in tandem with many of the other reading standards within the same grade, as students should continually support their responses to text with specific details contained in that text. Such support, or text evidence, is emphasized in the Common Core across all grades. To help meet this standard, the questions teachers ask should be "text-based," in that students need to refer to the details in the book as the basis for their answers (Coleman & Pimentel, 2012, p. 7).

RL.1–3

Figure 2.2 | **Reading Literature Standards 1–3: Key Ideas and Details**

Kindergarten	Grade 1	Grade 2
RL.K.1 With prompting and support, ask and answer questions about key details in a text.	**RL.1.1** Ask and answer questions about key details in a text.	**RL.2.1** Ask and answer **such** questions **as who, what, where, when, why, and how to demonstrate understanding of** key details in a text.
RL.K.2 With prompting and support, retell familiar stories, including key details.	**RL.1.2** Retell stories, including key details, **and demonstrate understanding of their central message or lesson.**	**RL.2.2** Recount stories, **including fables and folktales from diverse cultures**, and **determine** their central message, lesson, **or moral.**
RL.K.3 With prompting and support, identify characters, settings, and major events in a story.	**RL.1.3 Describe** characters, settings, and major events in a story, **using key details.**	**RL.2.3** Describe **how characters in a story respond to major events and challenges.**

Note: Boldface text identifies content that differs from the prior grade level.

This first reading standard describes a continuum of advancing skill linked to students' ability to ask and answer questions about books. As with all of the kindergarten-level standards under the Key Ideas and Details heading, it includes the phrase "with prompting and support," an acknowledgment that children this age may still require some assistance when called upon to demonstrate mastery. It's expected, for example, that kindergarten teachers may need to give students hints to help them remember a key detail in the story or that they may need to explain particular words or details in a text. The need for such supports lessens as reading comprehension improves, and this is reflected in the progression of the reading standards. By the end of 1st grade, it's expected that most students will be able to ask and answer questions independently. In 2nd grade, the types of questions that students are expected to ask and answer become more varied. As students move through the upper elementary grades, Reading Standard 1 focuses on developing their ability to draw inferences and support their questioning with specific references to the text.

For an example of a 1st grade lesson addressing Reading Literature Standard 2 (RL.1.2), please see **Sample Lesson 2.**

The second standard in Key Ideas and Details, Reading Literature Standard 2 (RL.2), addresses understanding the central theme in a book and the details that support it. In early elementary grades, students must show that they comprehend the essential details of what they hear or read through retelling, which is a precursor to the summarizing they will do in later grades. Again, it's acknowledged that kindergarten students will likely need some support when recounting the details of a story. In 1st grade, students are expected to understand the central message or lesson in the story in addition to retelling the details, and, in 2nd grade, they must be able to identify the moral of a cultural fable or folktale. As students progress through the upper elementary grades, they are asked to build on these earlier skills by clearly linking the details in a text to the central message and by exploring more complex messages, or themes, in works of fiction.

Across grades, the third standard in Key Ideas and Details, Reading Literature Standard 3 (RL.3), focuses on understanding story elements and how they work together. The standard for kindergarten focuses on identifying who the characters are, where the story takes place, and what happens, acknowledging that kindergarteners may need some guiding questions or other support to correctly identify these story elements. In 1st grade, students are expected to be able to describe these same elements and tie them to details in the text without support from others. In 2nd grade, the standard requires more analysis, as students make connections between a character's actions, words, or feelings and what happens in the story.

Figure 2.3 shows the sequence of standards for Key Ideas and Details within the Reading Informational Text domain. As described later in this chapter, the Common Core standards promote the reading of informational texts that support students' learning in other subject areas. This first heading in Reading Informational Text organizes standards that describe students' ability to comprehend the factual information and ideas in texts that they hear or read.

RI.1–3

Figure 2.3 | **Reading Informational Text Standards 1–3: Key Ideas and Details**

Kindergarten	Grade 1	Grade 2
RI.K.1 With prompting and support, ask and answer questions about key details in a text.	RI.1.1 Ask and answer questions about key details in a text.	**RI.2.1** Ask and answer **such questions as who, what, where, when, why, and how to demonstrate understanding of key details in a text**.
RI.K.2 With prompting and support, identify the main topic and retell key details of a text.	RI.1.2 Identify the main topic and retell key details of a text.	**RI.2.2** Identify the main topic of a **multi-paragraph text as well as the focus of specific paragraphs within the text**.
RI.K.3 With prompting and support, describe the connection between two individuals, events, ideas, or pieces of information in a text.	RI.1.3 Describe the connection between two individuals, events, ideas, or pieces of information in a text.	**RI.2.3** Describe the connection between a **series of historical events, scientific ideas or concepts, or steps in technical procedures in a text**.

Note: Boldface text identifies content that differs from the prior grade level.

As previously noted, Reading Informational Text Standard 1 (RI.1) is identical to the first standard in Reading Literature (RL.1), building students' ability to ask and answer questions about key details in a text. While it's expected that kindergarten students may need prompting and support, 1st grade students should be capable of some independent questioning, and by the end of 2nd grade, students are expected to be able to generate and answer a variety of questions about informational texts.

Reading Informational Text Standard 2 (RI.2) is similar to its counterpart in Reading Literature, except that students must retell information rather than a story. As with the Reading Literature standards, students progress from needing some prompting and support to identify the topic of the book and retell key details in kindergarten, to identifying and retelling details independently by the end of 1st grade. In 2nd grade, students learn to identify the focus or topic for each individual paragraph and determine the main idea of the entire piece. Understanding how information is structured by paragraphs will improve students' grasp of how details support the main points and also help students understand how to organize information in their own writing, such as using topic sentences to focus paragraphs.

For an example of a kindergarten lesson addressing Reading Informational Text Standard 2 (RI.K.2), please see **Sample Lesson 1.**

Reading Informational Text Standard 3 (RI.3) focuses on the specific relationships and connections among a variety of details within a text. Students explore relationships, such as cause and effect or sequence, to make connections among individuals, events, ideas, or pieces of information in the books that they read and that are read to them. To promote mastery of this standard, teachers may ask students specific questions designed to get them thinking about possible relationships. As is the case with the other standards under the Key Ideas and Details heading, it's acknowledged that kindergarten students may need their teacher to prompt them or provide supporting information to help them describe the connections between two details in a book. First graders are expected to make more connections independently. By 2nd grade, students are expected to be able to link more than two details by describing the connections among multiple aspects of the text. For example, they might compare details about each planet after reading about our solar system or describe the sequence of steps in a set of instructions.

As students progress into 3rd grade and beyond, they become more aware of the types of relationships and structures that occur in informational texts and are increasingly able to describe relationships using language that pertains to time, sequence, and cause/effect. In addition, the complexity of the ideas and information being studied steadily increases as the reading material and subject matter become more complex, which increases the difficulty of Reading Standard 3 over the course of students' schooling.

Reading strategies

Notably, the reading standards do not specify the use of particular reading comprehension strategies (such as making predictions), as was common in many state standards documents. The Common Core publishers' criteria document explains that

> To be effective, strategies should be introduced and exercised when they help clarify a specific part of a text and are dictated by specific features of a text and especially to assist with understanding more challenging sections. Over time, and through supportive discussion, interaction, and reflection, students need to build an infrastructure of skills, habits, knowledge, dispositions, and experience that enables them to approach new challenging texts with confidence and stamina. (Coleman & Pimentel, 2012, p. 9)

In other words, classroom teachers' instruction on particular reading strategies should be driven by the characteristics of particular books and by children's individual needs.

However, teachers will note that many skills commonly referred to as reading comprehension strategies are embedded within the Common Core standards. For example, the strategy of questioning is clearly required in Reading Standard 1 (RL.1 and RI.1). Strategies for determining the importance of information and ideas form part of Reading Standard 2 (RL.2 and RI.2), and making text-to-text connections is a key aspect of Reading Standard 3 (RL.3 and RI.3). Because many of the complex texts that students encounter in grades K–2 will be read aloud, teachers may find group reading activities to be an ideal time to model reflection and other reading strategies with a text that is above many of the students' current reading levels (see Reading Standard 10 on text complexity).

What the standards don't specify, however, are the reading strategies that students might apply. Teachers should use their best judgment about when and how to provide direct instruction on reading strategies. They should differentiate instruction on reading strategies to meet students' needs because young children come to school unevenly prepared and acquire reading skills at different rates. Teachers should also be sure to use available intervention systems when warranted and to always apply strategies and approaches in ways that are effective in the particular context of their classroom and their curriculum.

Craft and Structure

The standards under the Craft and Structure heading ask students to explain the techniques and strategies that authors use in texts, an understanding that not only supports students' close reading of texts but also serves as a model for their own writing. This heading organizes three standards, which ask students to analyze the word choice, organization, and point of view or purpose used in a text. Figure 2.4 shows the sequence of these standards for the Reading Literature domain. As you can see, there is almost no repetition across grade levels.

The first standard under this heading, Reading Literature Standard 4 (RL.4), emphasizes understanding authors' word choices. In kindergarten, students ask and answer questions about unknown words. In 1st grade, students study words that evoke particular feelings or sensations, and in 2nd grade, they explore the sounds of language—rhythm and rhyme. When students move into 3rd grade, RL.4 focuses on the difference between literal and nonliteral language; in 4th grade, its focus turns to words that stem from literary allusions, a topic that is addressed again and in depth in 8th grade. In 5th grade, the standard focuses on figurative language, such as metaphors and similes.

Figure 2.4 | **Reading Literature Standards 4–6: Craft and Structure**

Kindergarten	Grade 1	Grade 2
RL.K.4 Ask and answer questions about unknown words in a text.	**RL.1.4 Identify words and phrases in stories or poems that suggest feelings or appeal to the senses.**	**RL.2.4 Describe how** words and phrases **(e.g., regular beats, alliteration, rhymes, repeated lines) supply rhythm and meaning in a story, poem, or song.**
RL.K.5 Recognize common types of texts (e.g., storybooks, poems).	**RL.1.5 Explain major differences between books that tell stories and books that give information, drawing on a wide reading of a range of text types.**	**RL.2.5 Describe the overall structure of a story, including describing how the beginning introduces the story and the ending concludes the action.**
RL.K.6 With prompting and support, name the author and illustrator of a story and define the role of each in telling the story.	**RL.1.6 Identify who is telling the story at various points in a text.**	**RL.2.6 Acknowledge differences in the points of view of characters, including by speaking in a different voice for each character when reading dialogue aloud.**

Note: Boldface text identifies content that differs from the prior grade level.

Reading Literature Standard 5 (RL.5) addresses literary forms and genres, reflecting the belief that students should be exposed to a variety of types of literature and learn the characteristics of each. In kindergarten, students learn to recognize common text types, such as poetry and stories. In 1st grade, the focus is on differentiating fiction from nonfiction. In 2nd grade, students learn basic plot structure—beginning, middle, and end. With this groundwork established, students in upper elementary grades are prepared to examine more detailed characteristics of various literary genres.

Reading Literature Standard 6 (RL.6) concentrates on the point of view of various characters and narrators. Kindergarteners, given support, talk about the role of authors and illustrators. First graders learn to determine who is telling a story, and 2nd graders, to identify when the point of view or speaker changes. As with all of the reading comprehension standards, discussions about point of view should be grounded in a close review of examples and details in the story.

Figure 2.5 lists the standards under the Craft and Structure heading of the Reading Informational Text domain. While these standards mirror those under the same heading in Reading Literature, they include details specific to reading nonfiction. Again, there is very little repetition across grade levels.

RI.4–6

Figure 2.5 | **Reading Informational Text Standards 4–6: Craft and Structure**

Kindergarten	Grade 1	Grade 2
RI.K.4 With prompting and support, ask and answer questions about unknown words in a text.	**RI.1.4 Ask and answer questions to help determine or clarify the meaning of words and phrases in a text.**	**RI.2.4 Determine the meaning of words and phrases in a text relevant to a grade 2 topic or subject area.**
RI.K.5 Identify the front cover, back cover, and title page of a book.	**RI.1.5 Know and use various text features (e.g., headings, tables of contents, glossaries, electronic menus, icons) to locate key facts or information in a text.**	**RI.2.5** Know and use various text features (e.g., **captions, bold print, subheadings,** glossaries, **indexes,** electronic menus, icons) to locate key facts or information in a text **efficiently.**
RI.K.6 Name the author and illustrator of a text and define the role of each in presenting the ideas or information in a text.	**RI.1.6 Distinguish between information provided by pictures or other illustrations and information provided by the words in a text.**	**RI.2.6 Identify the main purpose of a text, including what the author wants to answer, explain, or describe.**

Note: Boldface text identifies content that differs from the prior grade level.

Reading Informational Text Standard 4 (RI.4) focuses on authors' word choices. When reading literature, students consider the emotional and figurative meaning of words and phrases, but when reading informational texts, their attention turns to the explicit meaning of words. In kindergarten, the standard is almost identical in Reading Literature and Reading Informational Text, with kindergarten students expected to learn new words by asking and answering questions about unknown words in a supportive environment, such as during group reading activities and discussions. The 1st grade standard centers on using questions to clarify the meaning of words and phrases. The 2nd grade standard emphasizes words and phrases that pertain to a specific subject area or topic, initiating a focus that continues throughout the higher grades. There is a clear connection between RI.4 and other standards in the Common Core that describe vocabulary skills; in particular, standards under the Vocabulary Acquisition and Use heading in the Language strand (see p. 70).

Reading Informational Text Standard 5 (RI.5) focuses on using the structures and organization of informational texts to locate information. Students begin work on this standard in kindergarten by identifying the front and back cover and title page of books. In 1st grade, they learn to use text features that organize content, such as the table of contents and glossaries. First graders also use features of digital media and computer software applications to locate information. In 2nd grade, students expand the types of text features that they use and come to employ familiar features with more ease.

For an example of a 2nd grade lesson addressing Reading Informational Text Standards 5, 6, and 7 (RI.2.5–7), please see **Sample Lesson 3.**

Reading Informational Text Standard 6 (RI.6) focuses on understanding texts' purpose and author's point of view. At the kindergarten level, this standard is very similar across the Reading Literature and Reading Informational Text domains: kindergarteners must define the role of authors and illustrators in creating a text. In 1st grade, RI.6 asks students to compare a text's illustrations with its written information, and in 2nd grade, it asks them to identify the author's purpose. As

For an example of a kindergarten lesson addressing Reading Informational Text Standard 6 (RI.K.6), please see **Sample Lesson 1.**

students move through the upper elementary grades, they will extend these skills further by exploring diverse perspectives and points of view.

Integration of Knowledge and Ideas

The standards under the Integration of Knowledge and Ideas heading focus on comparison of ideas and information from different works, including art and media. Reading Standards 7 and 9 appear within both the Reading Literature and Reading Informational Text domains, while Standard 8 appears only in Reading Informational Text (see our discussion on p. 30). Figure 2.6 shows the sequence of standards in Reading Literature.

Reading Literature Standard 7 (RL.7) describes how visual images and multimedia sources support comprehension of stories and create meaning. The standard at the kindergarten level is nearly identical to its counterpart

RL.7 & RL.9

Figure 2.6 | **Reading Literature Standards 7 and 9:**
Integration of Knowledge and Ideas

Kindergarten	Grade 1	Grade 2
RL.K.7 With prompting and support, describe the relationship between illustrations and the story in which they appear (e.g., what moment in a story an illustration depicts).	**RL.1.7 Use illustrations and details in a story to describe its characters, setting, or events.**	RL.2.7 Use **information gained from** the illustrations **and words in a print or digital text to demonstrate understanding of** its characters, setting, **or plot.**
[R.8 is not applicable to literature.]		
RL.K.9 With prompting and support, compare and contrast the adventures and experiences of characters in familiar stories.	**RL.1.9 Compare and contrast the adventures and experiences of characters in stories.**	RL.2.9 Compare and contrast **two or more versions of the same story (e.g., Cinderella stories) by different authors or from different cultures.**

Note: Boldface text identifies content that differs from the prior grade level.

in the Reading Informational Text domain, differing only in the example provided. In Reading Literature, kindergarteners make connections between a story's illustrations and its written words. For example, they may listen to a story read aloud and match the characters described in words to the characters depicted in the illustrations. First and 2nd graders can demonstrate their comprehension of texts by referring to illustrations and details in the text when talking about the story. When students reach upper elementary school, they will extend these skills by analyzing the effects of different media and formats on meaning.

Reading Literature Standard 9 (RL.9) asks students to compare characters and stories. The focus of the kindergarten and 1st grade standard is on comparing and contrasting the adventures and experiences of characters in stories. Kindergarten students are likely to need support from teachers, such as prompting questions or information, while 1st graders are expected to do the same work more independently. In 2nd grade, students go on to compare multiple versions of the same story; these comparisons can highlight choices that the authors and illustrators have made. To support effective comparison, curricular units of study should provide students with opportunities to read and link a variety of related works. This standard requires students to make connections within and between texts, which is a well-known strategy for aiding reading comprehension. When teaching Reading Standard 9, teachers may pair fiction and informational texts, allowing students to encounter and talk about different treatments of the same theme or topic.

Figure 2.7 lists the standards under the Integration of Knowledge and Ideas heading for Reading Informational Text. Similar to the standards under the same heading for Reading Literature, these standards focus on comparison and synthesis of ideas and information from different works and media, but the Reading Informational Text domain also includes a standard aimed at identifying reasons and support in works that express an opinion.

Reading Informational Text Standard 7 (RI.7) asks students to use illustrations and images to understand the meaning of informational texts. As previously described, the standard for kindergarten is nearly identical to the corresponding standard in the Reading Literature domain. Kindergarten

For an example of a kindergarten lesson addressing Reading Informational Text Standard 7 (RI.K.7), please see **Sample Lesson 1.**

students, with supporting input from their peers or teacher, are asked to describe how the illustrations in a book relate to the meaning of the text. The 1st grade standard is also nearly identical to its counterpart in the Reading Literature domain. Rather than using illustrations and text details to describe a book's setting or characters, however, students must use them to describe key ideas. Second grade students must understand the purpose of specific images in a text and determine how these images help a reader understand the information in that book or article. In grades 3–5, students will be asked to apply these same skills when examining a wider range of non-print texts, including graphic illustrations and multimedia.

Reading Informational Text Standard 8 (RI.8) appears only in the Reading Informational Text domain. This standard relates to understanding the evidence that an author provides to support his or her major points. It lays the foundation for standards in later grades that focus on evaluating logical arguments, which is a key aspect of the Common Core. Students in grades K–2 are asked to examine the ways in which authors support the points they make in informational texts. Students will likely need some scaffolding in kindergarten, but they are expected to use this skill more independently by the end of 1st grade. In 2nd grade, they are asked to link specific points the author makes to the supporting reasons for each point. By closely studying the ideas and supporting details in texts, students will gain a better understanding of how to develop their own ideas when writing or speaking.

The final standard in Integration of Knowledge and Ideas, Reading Informational Text Standard 9 (RI.9), is similar to its counterpart in Reading Literature, in that students must make connections within and between texts. Students are asked to identify basic similarities and differences between two books on the same topic with support (kindergarten) or more independently (1st grade). In 2nd grade, the standard focuses on comparing the key ideas within two books on the same topic. Across grades, this standard asks students to build knowledge on a subject by investigating different perspectives on the topic in diverse sources.

Figure 2.7 | **Reading Informational Text Standards 7–9:
Integration of Knowledge and Ideas**

Kindergarten	Grade 1	Grade 2
RI.K.7 With prompting and support, describe the relationship between illustrations and the text in which they appear (e.g., what person, place, thing, or idea in the text an illustration depicts).	**RI.1.7 Use the** illustrations **and details in a text to describe its key ideas.**	**RI.2.7 Explain how specific images (e.g., a diagram showing how a machine works) contribute to and clarity a text.**
RI.K.8 With prompting and support, identify the reasons an author gives to support points in a text.	**RI.1.8** Identify the reasons an author gives to support points in a text.	**RI.2.8 Describe how** reasons support specific points the author makes in a text.
RI.K.9 With prompting and support, identify basic similarities in and differences between two texts on the same topic (e.g., in illustrations, descriptions, or procedures).	**RI.1.9** Identify basic similarities in and differences between two texts on the same topic (e.g., in illustrations, descriptions, or procedures).	**RI.2.9** Compare and contrast **the most important points** presented by two texts on the same topic.

Note: Boldface text identifies content that differs from the prior grade level.

Range of Reading and Level of Text Complexity

The final standard in the Reading strand, Reading Standard 10 (RL.10/RI.10), describes the range and complexity of student reading materials to which the other reading standards for literature and informational text apply. The standard reflects the idea that students should read texts that increase in complexity each year. The Common Core text complexity model includes three factors: Quantitative Measures, Qualitative Measures, and Reader and Task Considerations. These factors are described in detail within Appendix

A to the ELA/literacy standards document (CCSSI, 2010d); models for each grade range are provided in Appendix B (CCSSI, 2010e).

The three factors work together to help teachers identify texts that are sufficiently complex for their students. In some cases, teachers may decide that one of the factors is more critical than the others in determining the appropriate grade level for a given text. For example, it may be determined that the topics or subject matter in a book indicate its Qualitative Measure and Reader and Task Considerations fit the complexity level for grades 4–5, while the Quantitative Measure for the same book indicates that it fits the complexity level for grades 2–3. Teachers should carefully consider each factor to decide the most appropriate grade placement for a given book or story. Rubrics have been developed by the Kansas State Department of Education (2011) and the National Center for the Improvement of Educational Assessment (Hess & Hervey, 2011) to help teachers assess Qualitative Measures and Reader and Task Considerations for both literature and informational text.

The level of complexity needed to keep students on the trajectory for college and career is described in text complexity grade bands, the first of which is for grades 2–3. By the time students complete 2nd grade, they should be reading texts that meet the criteria of this band, with teachers providing scaffolding, such as guided reading, as needed. Students in grades K–2 are, of course, still learning to read, and they will attain fluency and comprehension skills at different rates. Although reading programs should encourage independent reading of books matched to students' interests and reading levels, all students should also engage with complex texts through oral and group reading activities. Exposure to texts that are more difficult than students can read on their own is a way to build subject-area knowledge and language skills, including vocabulary knowledge.

Figure 2.8 shows the Range of Reading and Level of Text Complexity standard for Reading Literature (RL.10).

In addition to describing text complexity, Reading Literature Standard 10 addresses the range of student reading by identifying a variety of genres that students should read, including stories, dramas, and poetry. Stories appropriate to grades K–5 are further defined as children's adventure stories, folktales, legends, fables, fantasy, realistic fiction, and myth. Drama includes dialogue and brief dramatic scenes that depict settings familiar to students. Poetry includes nursery rhymes and the subgenres of the narrative poem, limerick, and free verse poetry (CCSSI, 2010c, p. 31).

RL.10

Figure 2.8	**Reading Literature Standard 10:** **Range of Reading and Level of Text Complexity**		
Kindergarten	Grade 1	Grade 2
RL.K.10 **Actively engage in group reading activities with purpose and understanding.**	RL.1.10 **With prompting and support, read prose and poetry of appropriate complexity for** *grade 1.*	RL.2.10 **By the end of the year, read and comprehend literature, including stories** and poetry, in the *grades 2–3 text complexity band* **proficiently, with scaffolding as needed at the high end of the range.**

Note: Boldface text identifies content that differs from the prior grade level.

Figure 2.9 shows the standards under the Range of Reading and Level of Text Complexity heading within Reading Informational Text.

This standard mirrors Reading Literature Standard 10, using identical phrasing to describe text complexity and the range of student reading of informational texts.

The types of informational texts that students should read in grades K–5 are defined as literary nonfiction and historical, scientific, and technical texts. These include biographies and autobiographies; books about history, social studies, science, and the arts; technical texts, such as directions, forms, and information display in graphs, charts, or maps; and digital sources on a range of topics. Although literary nonfiction includes genres that are structured similarly to narratives, such as biographies, the

RI.10

Figure 2.9 | **Reading Informational Text Standard 10:**
Range of Reading and Level of Text Complexity

Kindergarten	Grade 1	Grade 2
RI.K.10 Actively engage in group reading activities with purpose and understanding.	**RI.1.10 With prompting and support, read informational texts appropriately complex for *grade 1*.**	**RI.2.10** By the end of the year, read and **comprehend** informational texts, **including history/ social studies, science, and technical texts, in the *grades 2–3 text complexity band* proficiently**, with scaffolding as needed at the high end of the range.

Note: Boldface text identifies content that differs from the prior grade level.

standards emphasize nonfiction built on informational text structures, such as science or social studies topic books.

The standard in Range of Reading and Level of Text Complexity has clear implications for curriculum and instruction. It calls for teachers to select a variety of reading materials around topics or themes in order to systematically develop student knowledge. The standards document states that "within a grade level, there should be an adequate number of titles on a single topic that would allow children to study that topic for a sustained period" (CCSSI, 2010c, p. 33). What students learn through their reading and listening should be part of their study of history/social studies, science, and the arts and linked to the curriculum in those areas.

While Reading Standard 10 (RL.10/ RI.10) is clear that all students should hear or read complex texts, students also need opportunities to build fluency and vocabulary with texts matched to their individual reading levels and interests, that is, engaging books that they can comprehend independently.

Reading fluency is described further in the Reading Foundational Skills domain, the subject of the next chapter.

CHAPTER 3

Reading Foundational Skills

As its name implies, this domain within the Common Core's Reading strand contains standards focused on the foundational skills that children need when learning how to read. The authors of the Common Core standards note that "primary grade instruction in the foundations of reading is essential to ensure that reading problems are prevented and that most students will read well enough to benefit from grade level instruction" (Coleman & Pimentel, 2012, p. 1). The Reading Foundational Skills domain of the Common Core (also called "Foundational Skills" and abbreviated as RF) outlines specific early reading skills that provide the basis for students' learning across the curriculum and throughout their lives. Unlike all other standards in the Common Core for ELA/literacy, the standards in this domain are not directly associated with College and Career Readiness Anchor (CCRA) standards, and they do not extend past 5th grade. The bulk of the Foundational Skills standards are concentrated here, in the primary grades (K–2), although phonics and fluency remain a focus in grades 3–5.

The Foundational Skills standards are highly specific, providing guidance on the types of reading activities that should be incorporated into early learning classrooms. The Common Core publishers' criteria for K–2 recommends that curriculum materials "provide explicit and systematic instruction and diagnostic supports in concepts of print, phonological awareness, phonics, vocabulary development, syntax, and fluency" (Cole-man & Pimentel, 2012, p. 3). Of these topics, vocabulary and syntax are described in the Language strand (see Chapter 6), but all other topics are addressed here, in Foundational Skills.

The Foundational Skills domain organizes early reading skills under four headings: Print Concepts, Phonological Awareness, Phonics and Word Recognition, and Fluency. There is only one standard under each heading, which explains why it's common to hear reference to "*the* Print Concepts standard" or "*the* Phonological Awareness standard" for a given grade level. However, as noted, most of these standards are very specific, with a num-ber of detailed lettered subparts, or components.

Figure 3.1 provides an overview of the Foundational Skills domain at the lower elementary level.

Figure 3.1 | **The Reading Foundational Skills Domain: Grades K–2 Overview**

Heading	Kindergarten Standards	Grade 1 Standards	Grade 2 Standards
Print Concepts	RF.K.1	RF.1.1	—
Phonological Awareness	RF.K.2	RF.1.2	—
Phonics and Word Recognition	RF.K.3	RF.1.3	RF.2.3
Fluency	RF.K.4	RF.1.4	RF.2.4

Note: There are no CCRA standards associated with the Reading Foundational Skills domain. Standards for Print Concepts and Phonological Awareness conclude in grade 1.

In this chapter, we will describe each heading in the Foundational Skills domain and look at the components of its associated standard at all appli-cable grade levels.

Print Concepts

Print concepts refers to an understanding of what print represents and how it works—in other words, the understanding that printed text is speech that has been "written down" in a consistent manner and needs to be approached in a certain way.

As shown in Figure 3.2, Print Concepts standards are set only for kindergarten and 1st grade. Indeed, the majority of the content within Print Concepts is addressed in kindergarten, covering basic understandings that students need in order to apply phonetic knowledge and decoding skills to words on a page in the subsequent primary grades.

Figure 3.2 | **Reading Foundational Skills Standard 1: Print Concepts**

Kindergarten	Grade 1
RF.K.1 Demonstrate understanding of the organization and basic features of print. a. **Follow words from left to right, top to bottom, and page by page.** b. **Recognize that spoken words are represented in written language by specific sequences of letters.** c. **Understand that words are separated by spaces in print.** d. **Recognize and name all upper- and lowercase letters of the alphabet.**	RF.1.1 Demonstrate understanding of the organization and basic features of print. a. **Recognize the distinguishing features of a sentence (e.g., first word, capitalization, ending punctuation).**

Note: Boldface text identifies content that differs from the prior grade level.

The first component of the Print Concepts standard at the kindergarten level (RF.K.1a) focuses on the directionality of print—reading words from left to right and pages from top to bottom. Directionality is typically something children pick up during their experiences reading with adults, and so observing whether or not kindergarten students turn the pages of a book correctly and follow a teacher's finger to track words across the page may provide teachers with some insight into students' prior experiences with print materials and indicate the extent of direct instruction on print concepts that is needed as well as any misconceptions that require correction.

For an example of a kindergarten lesson addressing Reading Foundational Skills Standard 1 (RF.K.1), please see **Sample Lesson 1.**

The second component of the kindergarten standard in Print Concepts (RF.K.1b) is related to the alphabetic principle, which is the general understanding that a word is created by a unique sequence of letters that represent the phonemes, or sounds, of the word. Many young children are not predisposed to grasp the alphabetic principle on their own; however, direct instruction on alphabet knowledge and identification of phonemes, or individual sounds in words, will encourage students' application of this principle (Byrne, 1998).

The third component of the kindergarten standard under the Print Concepts heading (RF.K.1c) focuses on distinguishing words. To attain this skill, students must recognize what a letter is and understand that words are made up of a group of letters. Possible approaches to instruction include asking children to sort letters and words into appropriate categories or pointing out spaces between words during big book or shared book experiences (Kosanovich & Verhagen, 2012).

The final component of the Print Concepts kindergarten standard (RF.K.1d) focuses on students knowing the names of uppercase and lowercase letter forms. Early childhood educators likely have an established repertoire of instructional activities that will address this standard, including matching games and letter cards.

Students extend their understanding of print concepts when they reach 1st grade. Foundational Skills Standard 1 (RF.1.1a) asks students to recognize the print features of a sentence—capitalization of the first word and ending punctuation. Learning that one pauses at a period is an important step in the development of reading fluency and comprehension, and understanding the print features of a sentence is a precursor to understanding the essential components that make a sentence complete, which students will be expected to master in 4th grade (L.4.1f).

Phonological Awareness

Phonemes are the individual sounds in spoken language, and learning to isolate, blend, and manipulate these sounds helps children learn to read (National Institute of Child Health and Human Development, 2000). Students begin by repeating rhymes in songs and poems, and gradually they are able to distinguish the sequence of all the sounds in individual words.

Similar to the Print Concepts standard, the Phonological Awareness standard (RF.2) is present only at the kindergarten and 1st grade levels. Beyond 1st grade, students are asked to apply their skills with phonemes to printed text, which is the focus of the Foundational Skills standards under the next heading, Phonics and Word Recognition. There are a number of detailed components for the Phonological Awareness standard, and they are unique to each grade level, as shown in Figure 3.3.

Figure 3.3 | **Reading Foundational Skills Standard 2: Phonological Awareness**

RF.2

Kindergarten	Grade 1
RF.2 Demonstrate understanding of spoken words, syllables, and sounds (phonemes).	**RF.2** Demonstrate understanding of spoken words, syllables, and sounds (phonemes).
a. **Recognize and produce rhyming words.** b. **Count, pronounce, blend, and segment syllables in spoken words.** c. **Blend and segment onsets and rimes of single-syllable spoken words.** d. **Isolate and pronounce the initial, medial vowel, and final sounds (phonemes) in three-phoneme (consonant-vowel-consonant, or CVC) words. (This does not include CVCs ending with /l/, /r/, or /x/.)** e. **Add or substitute individual sounds (phonemes) in simple, one-syllable words to make new words.**	a. **Distinguish long from short vowel sounds in spoken single-syllable words.** b. **Orally produce single-syllable words by blending sounds (phonemes), including consonant blends.** c. Isolate and pronounce initial, medial vowel, and final sounds (phonemes) in spoken **single-syllable words.** d. **Segment spoken single-syllable words into their complete sequence of individual sounds (phonemes).**

Note: Boldface text identifies content that differs from the prior grade level.

To support instruction on this standard, Appendix A to the Common Core ELA/literacy standards provides a common progression of phonological awareness skills for grades preK–1 and phoneme awareness skills for grades K–2 (CCSSI, 2010d, pp. 18–19). These progressions list the most common sequence for attaining discrete oral language skills related to phonemes and provide examples for each skill. The components of RF.2 use the same order described in Appendix A's progressions. The progression for phonological awareness skills begins with distinguishing individual words and then moves on to recognizing rhymes, creating alliteration, identifying syllables, and manipulating onsets and rimes in spoken language. These skills reflect the components within RF.2 for kindergarten.

The progression of phoneme awareness skills continues with phoneme identification before moving on to phoneme isolation, blending, segmentation, addition, substitution, and deletion (see the standards document's Appendix A for examples of each skill). These skills are addressed primarily in the components of RF.2 for 1st grade. By the end of 1st grade, students should be able to apply their knowledge of phonemes (speech sounds) to their corresponding graphemes (printed letters and letter combinations), which is the focus of the standards under the domain's next heading, Phonics and Word Recognition.

Phonics and Word Recognition

Phonics teaches children about the relationship between phonemes and printed letters and how to apply this knowledge to reading and spelling. Explicit and systematic phonics instruction is correlated with improved reading skills (National Institute of Child Health and Human Development, 2000). The grade-level standards under this heading also address students' ability to recognize and decode words. Decoding is the ability to apply phonics and other letter knowledge in order to correctly pronounce written words.

To support instruction on phonics and decoding skills, Appendix A to the ELA/literacy standards provides a variety of reference tables and lists of common orthographic conventions, including consonant graphemes, types of syllable patterns, principles for syllabification, inflectional suffixes, and derivational suffixes (CCSSI, 2010d, pp. 17–22). These detailed resources support the Phonics and Word Recognition standard, Foundational Skills Standard 3 (RF.3), which is shown in Figure 3.4.

Similar to the other standards in this domain, the components of this standard are highly detailed and unique to each grade level. Unlike the standards under the first two headings in the Foundational Skills domain, the standards under this heading apply to each elementary grade, K–5.

In kindergarten, students begin to learn the most common sound for each letter and read high-frequency words. The types of sound-to-spelling correspondences that students learn expand over time and are detailed in the lettered components of RF.3 for each grade. In addition to knowing and applying grade-level phonics, students from 1st grade on are expected to be able to decode "grade-appropriate" words: described as single-syllable words in 1st grade and two-syllable words in 2nd grade with a few irregularly spelled words added in. Students also learn to segment words into syllables and apply knowledge of word parts (prefixes, root words, suffixes), such as inflectional endings, when decoding words. They will continue to practice these decoding skills in the upper elementary grades, gaining familiarity with all letter–sound correspondences, syllable patterns, and common word parts.

> For an example of a kindergarten lesson addressing a specific component of Reading Foundational Skills Standard 3 (RF.K.3c), please see **Sample Lesson 1.**

Fluency

The Fluency standard, Foundational Skills Standard 4 (RF.4), describes students' reading automaticity. As the number of words that students recognize in print grows and their ability to quickly decode words improves, their reading becomes faster, more accurate, and more expressive. Improved reading fluency also allows students to read silently, which is significantly faster than reading orally. Gaining fluency requires time and practice, and so elementary teachers are encouraged to build in regular

RF.3

Figure 3.4 | **Reading Foundational Skills Standard 3: Phonics and Word Recognition**

Kindergarten	Grade 1	Grade 2
RF.K.3 Know and apply grade-level phonics and word analysis skills in decoding words.	RF.1.3 Know and apply grade-level phonics and word analysis skills in decoding words.	RF.2.3 Know and apply grade-level phonics and word analysis skills in decoding words.
a. **Demonstrate basic knowledge of one-to-one letter-sound correspondences by producing the primary or many of the most frequent sounds for each consonant.**	a. **Know the spelling-sound correspondences for common consonant digraphs.**	a. **Distinguish long and short vowels when reading regularly spelled one-syllable words.**
b. **Associate the long and short sounds with the common spellings (graphemes) for the five major vowels.**	b. **Decode regularly spelled one-syllable words.**	b. **Know spelling-sound correspondences for additional common vowel teams.**
c. **Read common high-frequency words by sight (e.g., *the, of, to, you, she, my, is, are, do, does*).**	c. **Know final *–e* and common vowel team conventions for representing long vowel sounds.**	c. **Decode regularly spelled two-syllable words with long vowels.**
d. **Distinguish between similarly spelled words by identifying the sounds of the letters that differ.**	d. **Use knowledge that every syllable must have a vowel sound to determine the number of syllables in a printed word.**	d. **Decode words with common prefixes and suffixes.**
	e. **Decode two-syllable words following basic patterns by breaking the words into syllables.**	e. **Identify words with inconsistent but common spelling-sound correspondences.**
	f. **Read words with inflectional endings.**	f. Recognize and read grade-appropriate irregularly spelled words.
	g. **Recognize and read grade-appropriate irregularly spelled words.**	

Note: Boldface text identifies content that differs from the prior grade level.

opportunities for student independent reading. Activities such as partner reading, choral reading, and repeated readings of short passages may also help improve students' reading fluency.

The standard for fluency is nearly identical across grades 1–5, although the complexity of texts that students should be able to read increases each year, as previously described in Reading Standard 10. As students expand their reading vocabulary and become more confident decoding words, their fluency with grade-appropriate texts will grow. Reading assessments that use standardized passages meant to evaluate a student's fluency level will continue to be helpful for pairing individual children with appropriate texts for independent reading and for targeting instruction for children who are not yet fluent, including students who are learning English.

Figure 3.5 shows the standards for Fluency in the Reading Foundational Skills domain.

The kindergarten standard for fluency (RF.K.4) reflects the fact that kindergarteners are just beginning to decode words. They are asked to read emergent-reader texts with purpose and understanding, which might include activities such as reciting patterns from familiar books. In 1st and 2nd grades, students are asked to further their fluency by reading grade-appropriate texts with purpose and understanding, by

For an example of a 1st grade lesson addressing Reading Foundational Skills Standard 4 (RF.1.4), please see **Sample Lesson 2.**

reading these texts accurately with appropriate rate and expression, and by learning to monitor their own reading processes and use strategies to self-correct. These skills may be evaluated by listening to students read aloud, and they are closely tied to a variety of reading comprehension strategies. For example, making predictions about a book's content before reading is one way a teacher might encourage students to read with a specific purpose; asking and answering questions during the reading process will teach them a useful approach to self-monitoring their reading comprehension; and applying vocabulary strategies (see Language Standard 4 [L.4], p. 70) will help students self-correct word recognition.

Figure 3.5 | **Reading Foundational Skills Standard 4: Fluency**		
Kindergarten	Grade 1	Grade 2
RF.K.4 Read emergent-reader texts with purpose and understanding.	**RF.1.4 Read with sufficient accuracy and fluency to support comprehension.** a. **Read on-level text with purpose and understanding.** b. **Read on-level text orally with accuracy, appropriate rate, and expression on successive readings.** c. **Use context to confirm or self-correct word recognition and understanding, rereading as necessary.**	**RF.2.4 Read with sufficient accuracy and fluency to support comprehension.** a. Read on-level text with purpose and understanding. b. Read on-level text orally with accuracy, appropriate rate, and expression on successive readings. c. Use context to confirm or self-correct word recognition and understanding, rereading as necessary.

Note: Boldface text identifies content that differs from the prior grade level.

Overall, the standards in the Common Core's Reading Foundational Skills domain provide guidance on the specific knowledge and skills that primary-level teachers should incorporate into lessons so that students will be able to decode automatically and read with appropriate fluency by the 3rd grade.

CHAPTER 4

Writing

The standards within the Common Core's Writing strand (W) focus on three types of writing: writing opinion pieces, writing about information, and writing stories. The standards also include skills related to writing processes, including using technology and participating in research activities. Taken together, the standards emphasize writing as a tool that develops children's critical thinking and learning across subject areas.

Within the strand, the standards are organized under four headings: Text Types and Purposes, Production and Distribution of Writing, Research to Build and Present Knowledge, and Range of Writing; however, the final heading, Range of Writing, does not begin until 3rd grade. Figure 4.1 provides an overview of the writing standards for grades K–2.

Our discussion of the writing standards will be organized by the topic headings.

Text Types and Purposes

Across all grades, the standards under the Text Types and Purposes heading address the three primary types of writing: writing about opinions (argumentation), writing about information (exposition), and writing to tell a story (narration). For the first two writing types, students learn to support

Figure 4.1 | **The Writing Strand: Grades K–2 Overview**

Heading	CCRA Standard	Kindergarten Standards	Grade 1 Standards	Grade 2 Standards
Text Types and Purposes	W.1	W.K.1	W.1.1	W.2.1
	W.2	W.K.2	W.1.2	W.2.2
	W.3	W.K.3	W.1.3	W.2.3
Production and Distribution of Writing	W.4	—	—	—
	W.5	W.K.5	W.1.5	W.2.5
	W.6	W.K.6	W.1.6	W.2.6
Research to Build and Present Knowledge	W.7	W.K.7	W.1.7	W.2.7
	W.8	W.K.8	W.1.8	W.2.8
	W.9	—	—	—
Range of Writing	W.10	—	—	—

Note: Standards W.4 and W.10 begin in grade 3. Standard W.9 begins in grade 4.

their opinion or a main idea in organized paragraphs. For the third writing type, students write a story organized by a sequence of events.

The writing activities that students engage in should be divided fairly evenly among these three writing types. The Common Core calls for the same balance of writing that is assessed on the National Assessment of Educational Progress. In elementary school, this percentage is 30 percent persuasive (opinion pieces), 35 percent informative, and 35 percent narrative (National Assessment Governing Board, 2010).

Although students are not required to adapt their writing to specific audiences and purposes until 3rd grade (Writing Standard 4), they should be encouraged to practice writing in response to a variety of prompts and texts. The Common Core publishers' criteria for grades K–2 states that "writing assignments should be varied and ask students to draw on their experience, on their imagination, and most frequently on the texts they encounter through reading or read-alouds" (Coleman & Pimentel, 2012, p. 9). Essentially, providing students with regular writing opportunities will help them develop the fundamental skills they need to express their personal ideas and content-area learning effectively.

Appendix C to the Common Core ELA/literacy standards provides two to three samples of student writing for each grade level (CCSSI, 2010f). The samples are accompanied by explanations of how they exemplify proficient writing for particular grades and text types.

The standards under the Text Types and Purposes heading indicate that kindergarten students will use a combination of drawing, dictating, and writing to compose different types of texts. Young children attain fine motor skills at different rates, and so it is important that their ability to correctly form letters and words does not hinder them from communicating ideas, information, and stories in print. Thus, drawing pictures and oral dictation should be provided as options for young children. (Information on skills that affect students' ability to write, such as printing letters and spelling, is found in the Language strand [see L.1 and L.2].)

The standards for Text Types and Purposes are shown in Figure 4.2.

In Writing Standard 1 (W.1), students write about their opinions on a topic or book. This standard lays the foundation for students to build more formal arguments, which they will begin to do in 6th grade. Appendix A to the ELA/literacy standards cites a variety of research that identifies writing arguments as a key skill required for college readiness; the writing standards build this skill from kindergarten through high school. Recognizing how opinions are supported is also part of the reading standards. Reading Informational Text Standard 8 (RI.8) asks students to identify the reasons that authors provide to support points in a text. As students learn to recognize opinions and support for opinions in texts that they read or hear, they will be better able to base their own opinions on facts and information.

To meet Writing Standard 1, kindergarten students name a topic or book and state an opinion or preference about it. Building on this skill, 1st

W.1–3

Figure 4.2 | **Writing Standards 1–3: Text Types and Purposes**		
Kindergarten	Grade 1	Grade 2
W.K.1 Use a combination of drawing, dictating, and writing to compose opinion pieces in which they tell a reader the topic or the name of the book they are writing about and state an opinion or preference about the topic or book (e.g., My favorite book is….).	**W.1.1 Write** opinion pieces in which they **introduce** the topic or name the book they are writing about, state an opinion, **supply a reason for the opinion, and provide some sense of closure.**	**W.2.1** Write opinion pieces in which they introduce the topic or book they are writing about, state an opinion, supply **reasons that support** the opinion, **use linking words (e.g., *because, and, also*) to connect opinion and reasons, and provide a concluding statement or section.**
W.K.2 Use a combination of drawing, dictating, and writing to compose informative/explanatory texts in which they name what they are writing about and supply some information about the topic.	**W.1.2** Write informative/explanatory texts in which they name a **topic,** supply some **facts** about the topic, **and provide some sense of closure.**	**W.2.2** Write informative/explanatory texts in which they **introduce** a topic, **use** facts and **definitions to develop points, and provide a concluding statement or section.**
W.K.3 Use a combination of drawing, dictating, and writing to narrate a single event or several loosely linked events, tell about the events in the order in which they occurred, and provide a reaction to what happened.	**W.1.3 Write narratives in which they recount two or more appropriately sequenced events, include some details regarding what happened, use temporal words to signal event order, and provide some sense of closure.**	**W.2.3** Write narratives in which they recount a **well-elaborated event or short sequence of events,** include details to **describe actions, thoughts, and feelings,** use temporal words to signal event order, and provide a sense of closure.
Note: Boldface text identifies content that differs from the prior grade level.		

graders not only name a topic or book but also introduce it in a sentence. First graders also add a supporting reason for their opinion and conclude the piece with a phrase or sentence. Second graders supply multiple reasons for their opinion, using conjunctions to link these reasons to their opinion statement. Improved organization of student writing and use of transitions continues as students move through elementary school.

Writing Standard 2 (W.2) addresses writing about information. Informative (explanatory) writing helps students think critically about what they've learned. Because students are asked to draw on source information for this kind of writing, this standard has a strong connection to the writing standards under the Research to Build and Present Knowledge heading, described later in this chapter. Writing about information also complements standards within the Common Core's Reading and Speaking and Listening strands that focus on students' acquisition of topical knowledge.

Similar to W.1, Writing Standard 2 asks kindergarten students to name a topic, but instead of stating an opinion about the topic, they must supply some information about it. First grade students are asked to supply facts about their stated topic and provide a sense of closure. Second grade students must further supply definitions about the topic and a concluding statement or section. In the upper elementary grades, students improve their abilities to organize their writing, use transition words and phrases, and select more precise language and words to express their intended meaning.

For an example of a kindergarten lesson addressing Writing Standard 2 (W.K.2), please see **Sample Lesson 1.**

The third type of writing described in Text Types and Purposes is storytelling (narration). Writing Standard 3 (W.3) asks students to write about experiences, either real or imaginary. In contrast to the first two writing types, storytelling is structured by time and place. This kind of writing may appear in a variety of formats, including narrative poems or short stories, and it may serve a variety of purposes, such as relating a personal experience or entertaining an audience with humor.

Narrative writing increases students' appreciation of the story elements they encounter when reading, such as characters and setting. Indeed, students learning how to tell a story may benefit from simultaneously practicing skills found under the Craft and Structure heading in the Reading Literature domain (RL.4–6). Narrative writing also provides students with the opportunity to express their personal ideas and experiences, which can help them engage more deeply in their learning.

At the kindergarten level, Writing Standard 3 asks students to tell a story with one or more events in chronological order and to provide a reaction to them. By the end of 1st grade, students are expected to provide some detail about two or more sequenced events and use transition words to signal changes in time or place. In 2nd grade, students focus on increasing the level of detail in their stories, including details about characters' actions, thoughts, and feelings. As students continue to build their narrative skill in 3rd grade, they will learn to more clearly introduce a situation, write dialogue, and provide greater detail in their descriptions.

For an example of a 1st grade lesson addressing Writing Standard 3 (W.1.3), please see **Sample Lesson 2.**

Production and Distribution of Writing

While the first group of standards in the Writing strand details the qualities and characteristics of different writing types, the remaining standards focus on writing processes. Those under the Production and Distribution of Writing heading (see Figure 4.3) focus specifically on revision and using technology.

The first standard under this heading, Writing Standard 4 (W.4), which requires students to adapt their writing for specific tasks and purposes (in grades 3–5) and audiences (in grades 4–5), is not addressed in grades K–2. This exclusion does not mean that primary students should not be asked to write for a variety of purposes or tasks; however, they are not yet expected to make specific choices in and adaptations to their writing based on particular contexts.

Writing Standard 5 (W.5) addresses the writing process directly. Although not all student writing requires multiple drafts, students do

Figure 4.3 | **Writing Standards 4–6: Production and Distribution of Writing**

Kindergarten	Grade 1	Grade 2
[W.4 is not applicable in kindergarten.]	[W.4 is not applicable in grade 1.]	[W.4 is not applicable in grade 2.]
W.K.5 With guidance and support from adults, respond to questions and suggestions from peers and add details to strengthen writing as needed.	**W.1.5** With guidance and support from adults, **focus on a topic,** respond to questions and suggestions from peers, and add details to strengthen writing as needed.	**W.2.5** With guidance and support from adults and peers, focus on a topic and strengthen writing as needed **by revising and editing.**
W.K.6 With guidance and support from adults, explore a variety of digital tools to produce and publish writing, including in collaboration with peers.	**W.1.6** With guidance and support from adults, **use** a variety of digital tools to produce and publish writing, including in collaboration with peers.	**W.2.6** With guidance and support from adults, use a variety of digital tools to produce and publish writing, including in collaboration with peers.

Note: Boldface text identifies content that differs from the prior grade level.

need practice revising and editing some of their work. In grades K–2, it's expected that they will receive guidance and support from adults to help them improve the quality of their writing. Across the primary grades, Writing Standard 5 asks students to respond to questions and suggestions from their peers to identify ideas that they should elaborate on in a revised draft of their written work. In addition, students are asked to revise their writing to ensure that it has a clear focus (1st grade) and edit their writing to improve their use of grammar and conventions (2nd grade). Details about expectations for students' use of grammar and conventions are found in the Language strand (see Chapter 6).

Writing Standard 6 (W.6) describes how children will use technology to produce and publish writing and collaborate with others. This standard is nearly the same across grades K–2, except that the kindergarten standard asks these youngest students to simply explore the digital tools that 1st and 2nd grade students are expected to use in support of their writing efforts. As with W.5, it's important that students receive guidance and support as they work to meet this standard. Clearly, they will need direct instruction and help with any technical tools that are new to them. Also, students' familiarity with technology may vary widely, meaning teachers will need to focus on providing the degree of support that is needed by each individual student. The types of digital tools available will also vary significantly, but teachers should use all of the appropriate technology that is available to their classroom.

Writing Standard 6 expands in the upper elementary grades, where students are expected to be able to use technology to interact with peers (3rd grade) and use the Internet (4th grade). A primary focus for this standard in grades 3–5 is on developing keyboarding skills.

Research to Build and Present Knowledge

The research standards in the Common Core describe a set of skills that may be applied, as needed, to many different types of reading, speaking, and writing tasks. The standards under the Research to Build and Present Knowledge heading, shown in Figure 4.4, address the types of research projects appropriate for the primary grades and key skills such as gathering information from sources. The Research standards are largely the same across grade levels, although you will note that the final standard under this heading, which focuses on using source information to support analyses, doesn't begin until 4th grade.

Writing Standard 7 (W.7) describes the types of class research projects appropriate for these grades. The standard is uniform across grades K–2, differing only in the examples provided, which reflect children's growing ability to capture their learning in writing. Although the kindergarten example does not specify how students report their reactions to a set of books, 1st graders might synthesize their learning by drafting a set of instructions,

Figure 4.4 | Writing Standards 7–9: Research to Build and Present Knowledge

W.7–9

Kindergarten	Grade 1	Grade 2
W.K.7 Participate in shared research and writing projects (e.g., explore a number of books by a favorite author and express opinions about them).	**W.1.7** Participate in shared research and writing projects **(e.g., explore a number of "how-to" books on a given topic and use them to write a sequence of instructions).**	**W.2.7** Participate in shared research and writing projects **(e.g., read a number of books on a single topic to produce a report; record science observations).**
W.K.8 With guidance and support from adults, recall information from experiences or gather information from provided sources to answer a question.	**W.1.8** With guidance and support from adults, recall information from experiences or gather information from provided sources to answer a question.	**W.2.8** Recall information from experiences or gather information from provided sources to answer a question.
[W.9 is not applicable in kindergarten.]	[W.9 is not applicable in grade 1.]	[W.9 is not applicable in grade 2.]

Note: Boldface text identifies content that differs from the prior grade level.

and 2nd graders produce a simple report. These examples are not required activities, but they do provide a general sense of how students develop the ability to build knowledge about a topic and communicate this knowledge effectively. Students in upper elementary grades extend these skills by conducting independent research projects and using several sources.

Writing Standard 8 (W.8) states that students will recall information from their experiences or gather information in response to a question. This standard is the same across grade levels, except that 2nd grade students are expected to recall and gather information more independently than younger students. At all three primary grades, students are provided with research sources, such as books and magazines, related to the topic they

For an example of a 2nd grade lesson addressing Writing Standard 8 (W.2.8), please see **Sample Lesson 3.**

are studying. Teachers provide students with help finding relevant information, as needed. In upper elementary grades, students continue research work, learning to take notes independently and to sort information.

The final standard under Research to Build and Present Knowledge, Writing Standard 9 (W.9), does not begin until 3rd grade. It focuses on the ability of students to support their analysis of topics with text information.

Overall, the Common Core writing standards for the primary grades introduce students to the skills that will help them tell stories and respond to a variety of topics and texts in writing throughout their education. They learn how to include main ideas and details in their writing, how to use guidance and supportive writing tools, and how to draw information from sources.

CHAPTER 5

Speaking and Listening

The standards in the Common Core's Speaking and Listening strand (SL) address students' ability to engage in discussion, express their ideas orally, and listen to information presented by speakers or media. These skills play a particularly vital role in children's early learning. Appendix A to the ELA/ literacy standards states that "if literacy levels are to improve, the aims of the English language arts classroom, especially in the earliest grades, must include oral language in a purposeful, systematic way, in part because it helps students master the printed word" (CCSSI, 2010d, p. 26). In addition to laying a foundation for print literacy, speaking and listening skills allow children to engage with challenging texts across the curriculum that they are not yet able to access through independent reading. Listening to complex texts allows students to concentrate on the content and vocabulary without the need to decode.

In the classroom, students should work with a variety of texts and topics to practice their speaking and listening skills. As with the reading and writing standards, the speaking and listening standards should be used in conjunction with science, social studies, and other subject-area material and content. The speaking and listening standards may also be applied to the use of sign language for students who require adaptations (CCSSI, 2010b).

The standards within the Common Core's Speaking and Listening strand are divided under two headings: Comprehension and Collaboration, and Presentation of Knowledge and Ideas (see Figure 5.1).

Figure 5.1 | **The Speaking and Listening Strand: Grades K–2 Overview**

Heading	CCRA Standard	Kindergarten Standards	Grade 1 Standards	Grade 2 Standards
Comprehension and Collaboration	SL.1	SL.K.1	SL.1.1	SL.2.1
	SL.2	SL.K.2	SL.1.2	SL.2.2
	SL.3	SL.K.3	SL.1.3	SL.2.3
Presentation of Knowledge and Ideas	SL.4	SL.K.4	SL.1.4	SL.2.4
	SL.5	SL.K.5	SL.1.5	SL.2.5
	SL.6	SL.K.6	SL.1.6	SL.2.6

We'll review the standards under each heading separately.

Comprehension and Collaboration

The first standard under the Comprehension and Collaboration heading, Speaking and Listening Standard 1 (SL.1), focuses on discussion skills. This standard (see Figure 5.2) describes a variety of ways that children learn from each other during thoughtful academic conversations. It supports collaborative learning strategies and encourages teachers to create a variety of opportunities for students to discuss reading material or other topics being studied.

The detailed components within each grade level's version of SL.1 describe specific skills that will support successful student collaboration, such as taking turns when talking, contributing information to discussions, and asking questions about the information they hear. Students will likely practice the skills in this standard continually, as discussions are an integral part of instruction and learning in early grades. To encourage the development of students' conversational abilities, teachers should model and explicitly describe successful collaboration and discussion skills and acknowledge good discussion skills displayed by students during group activities.

Figure 5.2 | **Speaking and Listening Standard 1: Comprehension and Collaboration—Discussion**

SL.1

Kindergarten	Grade 1	Grade 2
SL.K.1 Participate in collaborative conversations with diverse partners about kindergarten topics and texts with peers and adults in small and larger groups.	**SL.1.1** Participate in collaborative conversations with diverse partners about **grade 1** topics and texts with peers and adults in small and larger groups.	**SL.2.1** Participate in collaborative conversations with diverse partners about **grade 2** topics and texts with peers and adults in small and larger groups.
a. **Follow agreed-upon rules for discussions (e.g., listening to others and taking turns speaking about the topics and texts under discussion).** b. **Continue a conversation through multiple exchanges.**	a. Follow agreed-upon rules for discussions (e.g., listening to others **with care, speaking one at a time** about the topics and texts under discussion). b. **Build on others' talk in conversations by responding to the comments of others** through multiple exchanges. c. **Ask questions to clear up any confusion about the topics and texts under discussion.**	a. Follow agreed-upon rules for discussions (e.g., **gaining the floor in respectful ways,** listening to others with care, speaking one at a time about the topics and texts under discussion). b. Build on others' talk in conversations by **linking their comments to the remarks of others.** c. Ask **for clarification and further explanation as needed** about the topics and texts under discussion.

Note: Boldface text identifies content that differs from the prior grade level.

To meet SL.1, students at all grade levels need opportunities to engage in varied types of structured discussions, including working in pairs and engaging in small- and large-group activities. Students in grades K–2 should learn and practice basic rules for discussion, such as listening quietly and taking turns when speaking. They also learn how to continue a conversation through multiple exchanges (kindergarten), build on the comments of others (1st grade), and link their comments directly to the remarks of others (2nd grade). Beginning in 1st grade, students also learn to monitor their own understanding, asking clarifying questions as needed. In grades 3–5, students will extend these skills by reading or preparing information in advance of a discussion, fulfilling an assigned role within a group, and drawing conclusions about the information and ideas shared in a discussion.

Speaking and Listening Standards 2 (SL.2) and 3 (SL.3), also under the Comprehension and Collaboration heading (see Figure 5.3), focus on listening skills. Listening is an important skill for students of all ages, but it plays a particularly important role in early education because students' receptive language abilities (understanding of oral or print messages) generally precede their expressive language abilities (communicating through speaking or writing). Children's first exposure to most words comes from hearing them; they later learn to recognize these words in printed text and to use them in their own speech. Appendix A to the ELA/literacy standards states that "the English language arts classroom should explicitly address the link between oral and written language, exploiting the influence of oral language on a child's later ability to read by allocating instructional time to building children's listening skills" (CCSSI, 2010d, p. 27). Because students in the primary grades are just learning to read, much of the information presented across subjects is communicated orally. Overall, reading fiction and content-rich texts aloud to students in grades K–2 will lay a strong foundation to support independent reading later on.

Speaking and Listening Standard 2 (SL.2) addresses understanding the key ideas in stories and information presented orally, including books read aloud and media sources such as videos. In response to spoken texts, students in kindergarten and 1st grade must ask and answer questions to show they understand the main ideas and key details. Second grade students are asked to retell stories or recount the main ideas of a spoken text. As students move through the upper elementary grades, they continue to improve their oral comprehension skills by summarizing and paraphrasing the main ideas and key details in oral text and diverse media.

SL.2–3

Figure 5.3 | **Speaking and Listening Standards 2–3: Comprehension and Collaboration—Listening**

Kindergarten	Grade 1	Grade 2
SL.K.2 Confirm understanding of a text read aloud or information presented orally or through other media by asking and answering questions about key details and requesting clarification if something is not understood.	**SL.1.2 Ask and answer** questions about key details **in a text read aloud or information presented orally or through other media.**	**SL.2.2 Recount or describe key ideas** or details from a text read aloud or information presented orally or through media.
SL.K.3 Ask and answer questions in order to seek help, get information, or clarify something that is not understood.	**SL.1.3 Ask and answer** questions about **what a speaker says in order to gather additional information** or clarify something that is not understood.	**SL.2.3 Ask and answer** questions about what a speaker says in order to **clarify comprehension,** gather additional information, **or deepen understanding of a topic or issue.**

Note: Boldface text identifies content that differs from the prior grade level.

Speaking and Listening Standard 3 (SL.3) is similar to the standard that directly precedes it. While the focus of SL.2 across grades is on understanding the content of diverse media and formats, the focus of SL.3 is on evaluating the information and ideas in spoken messages. In grades K–2, the standard is less analytic than it is in later grades, asking merely that students comprehend what a speaker says and be able to seek additional information from the speaker as needed. In kindergarten, students ask and answer questions for specific purposes—to seek help, get information, or clarify something not understood. Students extend these skills in grades 1 and 2, asking and answering questions specially about what a speaker has said in order to gather additional information (1st grade) and to extend their learning on a given topic (2nd grade). As their skills progress in elementary school, students assess spoken messages, identifying the evidence or reasons that support the speaker's main points.

Presentation of Knowledge and Ideas

The second topic heading in the Speaking and Listening strand is Presentation of Knowledge and Ideas. As its name implies, this group of three standards addresses oral presentation skills. It asks students to orally describe a story or information in detail, to use audio or visual aids, and to speak clearly, expressing complete thoughts. Figure 5.4 shows the sequence of standards under this heading across the primary grades.

Speaking and Listening Standard 4 (SL.4) focuses on the content and delivery of student presentations. Kindergarten students describe people, places, and things that are familiar to them, adding details in response to questions or prompting. First grade students are able to describe subjects that are not necessarily familiar; they are less likely to need prompting in order to provide adequate and relevant detail, and their expressions are expected to be more clearly stated than those of kindergarten students. Second grade students are asked to continue to improve the clarity of their speech, telling stories using audible and coherent sentences. While students in grades K–2 practice speaking through descriptions and storytelling, students in later elementary grades give organized presentations based on their personal opinions and on topics and texts they have studied.

Speaking and Listening Standard 5 (SL.5) focuses on using visual aids or audio recordings to support presentations. Students begin in kindergarten by creating simple drawings or other visual displays, like posters, which provide detail about a topic. In 1st grade, they learn to be more purposeful in selecting which details would benefit from illustration. Similar to the prior standard, SL.4, the focus of SL.5 in 2nd grade is storytelling. In addition to creating drawings and visual displays of their stories, 2nd graders are asked to create audio recordings of their stories or poems.

Figure 5.4 | **Speaking and Listening Standards 4–6:**
Presentation of Knowledge and Ideas

SL.4–6

Kindergarten	Grade 1	Grade 2
SL.K.4 Describe familiar people, places, things, and events and, with prompting and support, provide additional detail.	**SL.1.4 Describe people,** places, things, and events with **relevant details, expressing ideas and feelings clearly.**	**SL.2.4 Tell a story or recount an experience with appropriate facts** and relevant, **descriptive** details, **speaking audibly in coherent sentences.**
SL.K.5 Add drawings or other visual displays to descriptions as desired to provide additional detail.	**SL.1.5 Add drawings or** other visual displays to descriptions **when appropriate to clarify ideas, thoughts, and feelings.**	**SL.2.5 Create audio recordings of stories or poems;** add drawings or other visual displays to **stories or recounts of experiences** when appropriate to clarify ideas, thoughts, and feelings.
SL.K.6 Speak audibly and express thoughts, feelings, and ideas clearly.	**SL.1.6 Produce complete sentences when appropriate to task and situation.** (See *grade 1* Language standards 1 and 3 for specific expectations.)	**SL.2.6** Produce complete sentences when appropriate to task and situation **in order to provide requested detail or clarification.** (See *grade 2* Language standards 1 and 3 for specific expectations.)

Note: Boldface text identifies content that differs from the prior grade level.

Speaking and Listening Standard 6 (SL.6) focuses on the language children use when speaking. In kindergarten, students are asked to speak clearly and at an audible level. Beginning in 1st grade, they are expected to speak in complete sentences when appropriate and, in 2nd grade, to respond to questions or prompts with complete sentences when context requires. At the 1st and 2nd grade levels, SL.6 also directs teachers to the Language strand (see Chapter 6), which describes the grammatical skills students should attain in each grade as well as the necessary abilities to adapt speech to different contexts. Student presentations at each grade level should reflect the skills described in the Language strand.

In the Speaking and Listening strand, the Common Core describes students' oral communication skills in terms of interpersonal communication during discussions, the ability to express ideas orally, and listening skills. The standards also stress the important link between oral communication skills and students' overall literacy development.

CHAPTER 6

Language

The Language strand (L) focuses on skills related to standard English grammar and usage and vocabulary. Students study the language that authors and speakers use, and they practice using appropriate language in their own writing and speaking. Because the skills in this strand support skills described in the Reading, Writing, and Speaking and Listening strands, they are easily addressed in conjunction with other Common Core standards in curricular units and daily lessons.

Teachers of students who are learning English as a second language should note that "it is possible to achieve the standards for reading and literature, writing & research, language development and speaking & listening without manifesting native-like control of conventions and vocabulary" (CCSSI, 2010a, p. 1). Expectations for English language learners, particularly in regard to the language standards, will need to be adjusted based on individual assessment and monitoring of student progress.

The standards within this strand (see Figure 6.1) are organized under three headings: Conventions of Standard English, Knowledge of Language, and Vocabulary Acquisition and Use.

63

Figure 6.1	**The Language Strand: Grades K–2 Overview**			
Heading	CCRA Standard	Kindergarten Standards	Grade 1 Standards	Grade 2 Standards
Conventions of Standard English	L.1	L.K.1	L.1.1	L.2.1
	L.2	L.K.2	L.1.2	L.2.2
Knowledge of Language	L.3	—	—	L.2.3
Vocabulary Acquisition and Use	L.4	L.K.4	L.1.4	L.2.4
	L.5	L.K.5	L.1.5	L.2.5
	L.6	L.K.6	L.1.6	L.2.6

Note: Standard L.3 begins in grade 2.

Conventions of Standard English

There are two standards under the Conventions of Standard English heading. The first, Language Standard 1 (L.1), details grammar and usage conventions for both writing and speaking. The second, Language Standard 2 (L.2), lists specific rules related to capitalization, punctuation, and spelling in students' written work. The detailed components listed within these standards differ significantly from grade level to grade level, identifying distinct and specific skills that build students' understanding of and ability to use language effectively as they progress through their schooling.

Figure 6.2 shows the sequence of Language Standard 1 (L1) for grades K–2.

Language Standard 1, sometimes referred to as "the grammar and usage standard," describes a variety of specific grammatical constructions that students are expected to produce correctly in their speech or writing. Although students typically develop the ability to use different types of words, phrases, and sentences through exposure to oral and written

Figure 6.2 | **Language Standard 1:**
  Conventions of Standards English—Grammar and Usage

Kindergarten	Grade 1	Grade 2
L.K.1 Demonstrate command of the conventions of standard English grammar and usage when writing or speaking. a. **Print many upper- and lowercase letters.** b. **Use frequently occurring nouns and verbs.** c. **Form regular plural nouns orally by adding /s/ or /es/ (e.g., dog, dogs; wish, wishes).** d. **Understand and use question words (interrogatives) (e.g., who, what, where, when, why, how).** e. **Use the most frequently occurring prepositions (e.g., to, from, in, out, on, off, for, of, by, with).** f. **Produce and expand complete sentences in shared language activities.**	**L.1.1** Demonstrate command of the conventions of standard English grammar and usage when writing or speaking. a. Print **all** upper- and lowercase letters. b. **Use common, proper, and possessive nouns.** c. **Use singular and plural nouns with matching verbs in basic sentences (e.g., He hops; We hop).** d. **Use personal, possessive, and indefinite pronouns (e.g., I, me, my; they, them, their, anyone, everything).** e. **Use verbs to convey a sense of past, present, and future (e.g., Yesterday I walked home; Today I walk home; Tomorrow I will walk home).** f. **Use frequently occurring adjectives.** g. **Use frequently occurring conjunctions (e.g., and, but, or, so, because).**	**L.2.1** Demonstrate command of the conventions of standard English grammar and usage when writing or speaking. a. **Use collective nouns (e.g., group).** b. **Form and use frequently occurring irregular plural nouns (e.g., feet, children, teeth, mice, fish).** c. **Use reflexive pronouns (e.g., myself, ourselves).** d. **Form and use the past tense of frequently occurring irregular verbs (e.g., sat, hid, told).** e. **Use adjectives and adverbs, and choose between them depending on what is to be modified.** f. Produce, expand, and **rearrange** complete simple and compound sentences (e.g., *The boy watched the movie; The little boy watched the movie; The action movie was watched by the little boy*).

Note: Boldface text identifies content that differs from the prior grade level.

(continued)

Figure 6.2 | **Language Standard 1:**
Conventions of Standards English—Grammar and Usage (*continued*)

Kindergarten	Grade 1	Grade 2
	h. **Use determiners (e.g., articles, demonstratives).** i. Use frequently occurring prepositions (e.g., ***during, beyond, toward***). j. Produce and expand complete **simple and compound declarative, interrogative, imperative, and exclamatory sentences in response to prompts.**	

Note: Boldface text identifies content that differs from the prior grade level.

English, the use of some words and phrases, particularly those that are irregular or don't follow a pattern, may require direct instruction and targeted student practice.

For some skills in this standard, there is a clear progression from grade level to grade level. For example, kindergarteners are expected to form regular plural nouns, 1st graders are expected to match plural verbs with plural nouns (subject–verb agreement), and 2nd graders are expected to use frequently occurring irregular plural nouns (those that do not follow the normal pattern of adding *–s* or *–es*). In this way, the specific skills described in Language Standard 1 progress to build the complexity of students' grammar as they advance through school. Because the standards for grammar and conventions are so specific, teachers will need to review and adjust their curriculum resources across grades to ensure that they emphasize the skills that are a focus for their particular grade level.

In addition to the correct use of particular parts of speech and sentence types, Language Standard 1 addresses some expectations related to penmanship. Kindergarten students are asked to print *many* upper- and lower-case letters, while 1st grade students are asked to be able to print them all. The rate at which children gain this skill will depend largely on the development of their fine motor skills, which is highly variable. It is interesting that content related to penmanship does not extend past 1st grade and that cursive writing, which was fairly common in prior state standards around 3rd grade, is not a requirement in the Common Core.

Figure 6.3 shows the sequence of Language Standard 2 (L.2) within Conventions of Standard English, which is focused on print conventions and addresses specific capitalization, punctuation, and spelling rules. Similar to the grammar-focused standard that precedes it, Language Standard 2 has many detailed components describing specific skills for each grade level. The level of grade-by-grade specificity in both L.1 and L.2 can be a great help to teachers, alerting them not only to instructional targets for the current grade level but also to prerequisite skills they may find necessary to revisit.

Because grammar and conventions are encountered in all literacy contexts, instruction on and assessment of these skills may be integrated into a wide variety of classroom activities. For example, during a read-aloud of a big book, a teacher might point out punctuation and describe its purpose.

Language Standard 2 asks kindergarten students to write the letter(s) for consonant and short vowel sounds. As students move into 1st and 2nd grades, they continue to draw on phonetic knowledge, learn spelling patterns, and by the end of 2nd grade, learn how to consult reference materials to answer questions about spelling. There is a close relationship between the spelling content in this standard and content in RF.3, the standard under the Phonics and Word Recognition heading of the Reading Foundational Skills domain (see Chapter 3). In both, students make connections between the printed forms of letters (graphemes) and the letters' associated sounds (phonemes). The ability to make this connection is the basis of spelling (orthography) in writing, just as it is the basis for decoding

Figure 6.3 | **Language Standard 2:**
Conventions of Standards English—Conventions of Print

Kindergarten	Grade 1	Grade 2
L.K.2 Demonstrate command of the conventions of standard English capitalization, punctuation, and spelling when writing. a. **Capitalize the first word in a sentence and the pronoun *I*.** b. **Recognize and name end punctuation.** c. **Write a letter or letters for most consonant and short-vowel sounds (phonemes).** d. **Spell simple words phonetically, drawing on knowledge of sound-letter relationships.**	L.1.2 Demonstrate command of the conventions of standard English capitalization, punctuation, and spelling when writing. a. Capitalize **dates and names of people.** b. **Use end punctuation for sentences.** c. **Use commas in dates and to separate single words in a series.** d. **Use conventional spelling for words with common spelling patterns and for frequently occurring irregular words.** e. Spell **untaught words** phonetically, **drawing on phonemic awareness and spelling conventions.**	L.2.2 Demonstrate command of the conventions of standard English capitalization, punctuation, and spelling when writing. a. Capitalize **holidays, product names, and geographic names.** b. **Use commas in greetings and closings of letters.** c. **Use an apostrophe to form contractions and frequently occurring possessives.** d. **Generalize learned spelling patterns when writing words (e.g., *cage, badge; boy, boil*).** e. **Consult reference materials, including beginning dictionaries, as needed to check and correct spellings.**

Note: Boldface text identifies content that differs from the prior grade level.

in reading. Appendix A to the Common Core ELA/literacy standards provides lists of specific orthographic conventions that students should learn (CCSSI, 2010d, pp. 20–21).

Language Standard 2 also describes specific punctuation and capitalization rules that students should learn in each grade. Students are expected to recognize end punctuation (kindergarten), use end punctuation and commas in a series (1st grade), and punctuate contractions and letter openings/closings (2nd grade). They must learn to capitalize the beginning of sentences and "I" (kindergarten), dates and people's names (1st grade), and other proper nouns (2nd grade). Teachers may point out these conventions during read-alouds and should help students apply them in their own writing.

Knowledge of Language

There is just one standard under the Knowledge of Language heading (see Figure 6.4), and it describes students' ability to adapt their language to different contexts. The first time this standard appears is in 2nd grade.

Figure 6.4 | **Language Standard 3: Knowledge of Language**

L.3

Kindergarten	Grade 1	Grade 2
[L.3 is not applicable in kindergarten.]	[L.3 is not applicable in grade 1.]	**L.2.3 Use knowledge of language and its conventions when writing, speaking, reading, or listening.** a. **Compare formal and informal uses of English.**

Note: Boldface text identifies content that differs from the prior grade level.

Language Standard 3 (L.3) addresses children's understanding of how language is used for different purposes. In 2nd grade, the focus is on comparing formal and informal uses of English. For example, students may identify slang in the dialogue of a play or story and compare it to academic vocabulary used in a textbook or a piece of nonfiction. As students move on to the upper elementary and middle school grades, they will practice selecting words and phrases in their speech and writing that are appropriate for particular audiences and purposes.

Vocabulary Acquisition and Use

A significant body of research identifies vocabulary development as a key element for reading comprehension and academic success (National Institute of Child Health and Human Development, 2000). The Common Core standards for vocabulary in grades K–2 call for students to use strategies to comprehend words and phrases they encounter in texts, to understand word relationships and synonyms, and to expand their working vocabulary by studying unfamiliar words they encounter in complex literary and informational texts.

Teachers should support vocabulary acquisition in a variety of ways, as research tells us that combining multiple approaches to vocabulary instruction is more effective than any one strategy alone (National Institute of Child Health and Human Development, 2000). For example, introducing difficult vocabulary from a text before reading and multiple exposures to the same words are strategies that may be used together to strengthen students' overall vocabulary acquisition.

Figure 6.5 shows the sequence of standards under the Vocabulary Acquisition and Use heading. Teachers designing lessons that address vocabulary should note that the content under this heading is similar to content in Reading Standard 4 (RL.4/RI.4), which addresses comprehension of words and phrases in a text.

Language Standard 4 (L.4) describes the types of words that students will study and the strategies they'll undertake to comprehend those words. In kindergarten, students show that they understand common multiple-meaning words (homonyms) by using them correctly in different contexts. First grade students use sentence-level context as clues to the meaning of words, and 2nd grade students also use reference materials to learn words.

Using word parts appears as a vocabulary strategy in Language Standard 1 across the primary grades. Students learn how word parts indicate

Figure 6.5 | **Language Standards 4–6: Vocabulary Acquisition and Use**

Kindergarten	Grade 1	Grade 2
L.K.4 Determine or clarify the meaning of unknown and multiple-meaning words and phrases based on *kindergarten reading and content*. a. **Identify new meanings for familiar words and apply them accurately (e.g., knowing *duck* is a bird and learning the verb to *duck*).** b. **Use the most frequently occurring inflections and affixes (e.g., *–ed, –s, re–, un–, pre–, –ful, –less*) as a clue to the meaning of an unknown word.**	L.1.4 Determine or clarify the meaning of unknown and multiple-meaning words and phrases based on *grade 1 reading and content*, **choosing flexibly from an array of strategies.** a. **Use sentence-level context as a clue to the meaning of a word or phrase.** b. Use frequently occurring affixes as a clue to the meaning of a word. c. **Identify frequently occurring root words (e.g., *look*) and their inflectional forms (e.g., *looks, looked, looking*).**	L.2.4 Determine or clarify the meaning of unknown and multiple-meaning words and phrases based on *grade 2 reading and content*, choosing flexibly from an array of strategies. a. Use sentence-level context as a clue to the meaning of a word or phrase. b. **Determine the meaning of the new word formed when a known prefix is added to a known word (e.g., *happy/unhappy, tell/retell*).** c. **Use a known root word as a clue to the meaning of an unknown word with the same root (e.g., *addition, additional*).** d. **Use knowledge of the meaning of individual words to predict the meaning of compound words (e.g., *birdhouse, lighthouse, housefly, bookshelf, notebook, bookmark*).** e. **Use glossaries and beginning dictionaries, both print and digital, to determine or clarify the meaning of words and phrases.**

(continued)

L.4–6

Figure 6.5 | **Language Standards 4–6: Vocabulary Acquisition and Use (*continued*)**

Kindergarten	Grade 1	Grade 2
L.K.5 With guidance and support from adults, explore word relationships and nuances in word meanings. a. **Sort common objects into categories (e.g., shapes, foods) to gain a sense of the concepts the categories represent.** b. **Demonstrate understanding of frequently occurring verbs and adjectives by relating them to their opposites (antonyms).** c. **Identify real-life connections between words and their use (e.g., note places at school that are *colorful*).** d. **Distinguish shades of meaning among verbs describing the same general action (e.g., *walk, march, strut, prance*) by acting out the meanings.**	**L.1.5** With guidance and support from adults, **demonstrate understanding** of word relationships and nuances in word meanings. a. **Sort words into categories (e.g., colors, clothing) to gain a** sense of the concepts the categories represent. b. **Define words by category and by one or more key attributes (e.g., a *duck* is a bird that swims; a *tiger* is a large cat with stripes).** c. Identify real-life connections between words and their use (e.g., note places at home that are cozy). d. Distinguish shades of meaning among verbs **differing in manner (e.g., *look, peek, glance, stare, glare, scowl*) and adjectives differing in intensity (e.g., *large, gigantic*) by defining or choosing them or** by acting out the meanings.	**L.2.5** Demonstrate understanding of word relationships and nuances in word meanings. a. Identify real-life connections between words and their use **(e.g., describe foods that are *spicy* or *juicy*).** b. Distinguish shades of meaning among *closely related* verbs **(e.g., *toss, throw, hurl*) and closely** related adjectives **(e.g., *thin, slender, skinny, scrawny*).**

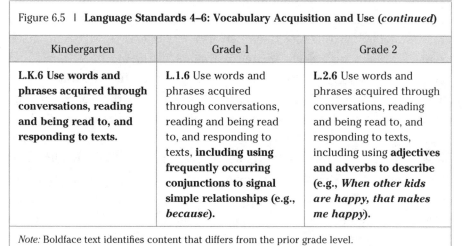

Figure 6.5 | **Language Standards 4–6: Vocabulary Acquisition and Use (*continued*)**   L.4–6

Kindergarten	Grade 1	Grade 2
L.K.6 Use words and phrases acquired through conversations, reading and being read to, and responding to texts.	**L.1.6** Use words and phrases acquired through conversations, reading and being read to, and responding to texts, **including using frequently occurring conjunctions to signal simple relationships (e.g., *because*).**	**L.2.6** Use words and phrases acquired through conversations, reading and being read to, and responding to texts, including using **adjectives and adverbs to describe (e.g., *When other kids are happy, that makes me happy*).**

Note: Boldface text identifies content that differs from the prior grade level.

meaning by studying frequently occurring inflections and affixes in kindergarten; frequently occurring affixes and root words in 1st grade; and prefixes, root words, and compound words in 2nd grade. In later grades, students will focus on Greek and Latin prefixes, suffixes, and root words. Although the study of word parts is associated with an increased vocabulary for all students, this approach will be particularly beneficial to children who are learning English as a second language and whose first language shares cognates with English as they learn to apply their first-language vocabulary knowledge when reading English (CCSSI, 2010a).

To teach students how to apply vocabulary strategies, teachers may model them by thinking aloud during group reading activities. For example, a teacher might point out how a word is related to its context while reading or guide students in determining a word's meaning by examining its parts.

The second standard focused on vocabulary acquisition and use, Language Standard 5 (L.5), targets the understanding of word relationships and subtle word meanings. The details and examples provided in the components of L.5 are specific to each grade level, helping to focus teachers' instruction and exposing students to a wide variety of figurative language and word relationships over the course of their schooling. In each grade, students build their understanding of word categories, such as synonyms and antonyms; make connections between words and real life; and make connections among closely related words. By studying how words and phrases are used in the texts that they read or hear, students will develop their ability to select effective language when they are writing and speaking.

The final standard under this heading, Language Standard 6 (L.6), addresses students' working vocabulary. In the primary grades, L.6 emphasizes acquiring words through conversation, listening, and reading and then using those words in their own speech and writing. Reading aloud to students the kinds of complex texts they may not be able to read independently allows for the introduction of all kinds of unfamiliar vocabulary words and phrases. The standard doesn't target any specific word types for kindergarteners; the expectation is simply for them to acquire words generally. First grade students, however, are asked to focus on words that signal simple relationships, and second graders, to focus on descriptive adjectives and adverbs.

Beginning in 3rd grade, Language Standard 6 focuses on academic and subject-specific vocabulary.

The Common Core language standards for the primary grades specify the nuts and bolts of language arts instruction. The skills in this strand cut across reading, writing, speaking, and listening tasks, articulating students' growing understanding of language constructions and their ability to apply those constructions to their own communication. The majority of these skills will be familiar to teachers; however, the Common Core may dictate details for each grade level that were not previously a focus for instruction.

PART II

Mathematics

CHAPTER 7

About the Common Core Mathematics Standards for Grades K–2

The Common Core mathematics standards are organized into two sets: the Standards for Mathematical Content, designed to cross traditional course boundaries and cover all the conceptual mathematical understanding necessary for students to develop from kindergarten through 12th grade, and the Standards for Mathematical Practice, which highlight the kinds of expertise that are essential for students to develop and use throughout this same grade span.

As we noted in Part I of this guide, the Common Core standards differ in many ways from most existing state standards documents, providing a greater level of detail about concepts, thought processes, and approaches. This level of detail often leads to much longer, more involved standards, some of which are up to a paragraph in length. Some of the mathematics standards detail conceptual methods of teaching and learning skills and concepts (e.g., combining data collection and representation with measurement, relating addition and subtraction to length) that are not typically explicit in other standards documents.

Another example of this detailed focus on the mental processes required to understand mathematical concepts is found in the set of Standards for Mathematical Practice, which receives the same level of emphasis as the Standards for Mathematical Content.

In this chapter, we will walk you through the standards' structure, provide an overview of how they work together, and offer some guidance on what to focus on as you begin your implementation efforts.

The Standards for Mathematical Content

In the elementary levels, the Standards for Mathematical Content are organized first by grade. Each grade level is introduced with a one- or two-page introduction, which consists of two parts—a summary of the three to four critical areas (topics) for each grade and an in-depth narrative description of those critical areas. Figure 7.1 provides a brief, grade-by-grade summary for kindergarten and grades 1 and 2.

In order to delve as deeply into each of these critical areas as the standards' degree of rigor requires, grade-level teachers should commit to spending the majority of their mathematics instructional time on these topics. This emphasis necessitates a reduced focus on other content. It also means teachers will need to cut customary curriculum topics that have been moved to a different grade level—a step that some teachers may be wary of taking, as it requires a baseline level of trust in the Common Core's grade-level progression of content. It's our hope that the discussion in Part II of this guide will help teachers gain an understanding of these progressions, allowing them to let go of mathematics content that is no longer a critical area or an area of support for their grade.

In the chapters to come, we will review each domain of the grades K–2 mathematics standards separately, providing an overview of its critical areas and illustrating how the content of each domain relates to the mathematical practices. We will then look at each cluster within the domain, identifying the connections among clusters and describing how the content differs and builds across grades. This close analysis will provide a clearer

Figure 7.1 | Critical Areas Within the Lower Elementary Domains by Grade Level

Domain Name	Kindergarten	Grade 1	Grade 2
Counting and Cardinality	• Counting up to 20 objects in a set • Counting out a given number of objects (up to 20) • Connecting counting to cardinality for a set of objects • Comparing sets of objects or numerals between 1 and 10	*Domain not addressed at this grade level*	*Domain not addressed at this grade level*
Operations and Algebraic Thinking	• Modeling simple joining and separating with sets of objects (within 10) • Counting the number of objects in a set after some are added or some are taken away (within 10)	• Using strategies for adding and subtracting whole numbers • Modeling add-to, take-from, put-together, take-apart, and compare problems • Applying the properties of addition to add and subtract whole numbers	• Demonstrating fluency with addition and subtraction within 20
Number and Operations in Base Ten	*No critical areas identified for this domain at this grade level*	• Adding two-digit numbers using strategies • Subtracting multiples of 10 • Comparing two two-digit numbers • Understanding place value to the tens place	• Counting in 5s, 10s, and multiples of 100s, 10s, and 1s • Understanding place values to the thousands • Fluently adding and subtracting within 100 using strategies • Solving addition and subtraction problems within 1000 • Mentally calculating sums and difference for numbers with only tens or only hundreds

(continued)

Figure 7.1 | **Critical Areas Within the Lower Elementary Domains by Grade Level (*continued*)**

Domain Name	Kindergarten	Grade 1	Grade 2
Measurement and Data	*No critical areas identified for this domain at this grade level*	• Underlying concepts of measurement (iterating, transitivity principle)	• Standard units of measure
Geometry	• Using geometric ideas and vocabulary (e.g., names of shapes, relative positions, two- or three-dimensional) to model and describe objects in their environment • Identifying, naming, and describing basic two- and three-dimensional shapes with different sizes and orientations • Constructing more complex shapes from simple shapes	• Composing and decomposing plane or solid figures	• Describing and analyzing shapes by examining their sides and angles • Composing and decomposing plane or solid figures

Note: Content in this table was adapted from the descriptions in the grade-level introductions within the mathematics standards document (CCSSI, 2010g).

understanding of the meaning of each standard within the context of the entirety of the Common Core standards for mathematics. We believe it will enhance teachers' understanding of how students have been prepared throughout the grades for each concept—insight they can use to reassure themselves of the appropriateness of the content their grade-level standards address and then apply during lesson planning to deliver more effective instruction and improve students' learning.

After the grade-level introductions, the standards within each grade are organized hierarchically, as follows:

- *Domain:* Expressed in a short phrase, a domain articulates big ideas that connect standards and topics. Elementary school standards for grades K–2 are categorized into five domains: Counting and Cardinality (CC), Operations and Algebraic Thinking (OA), Number and Operations in Base Ten (NBT), Measurement and Data (MD), and Geometry (G).

- *Cluster:* A cluster captures several ideas that, taken with all the other clusters within that domain, summarize the important aspects of mathematics students will encounter. For example, there are eight total clusters in the Operations and Algebraic Thinking domain in grades K–2: one for kindergarten, four for grade 1, and three for grade 2. The first of the 1st grade clusters in this domain (Cluster A) is "Represent and solve problems involving addition and subtraction." Content addressed in different domains and clusters may be closely related, reflecting the standards writers' emphasis on the interconnections throughout mathematics.

- *Standard:* A standard is a specific description of what students should understand and be able to do. It may be one sentence or several sentences long, and it sometimes includes lettered subsections. There is at least one and often several standards within every cluster. For example, at the 1st grade level, one of two standards under the cluster "Represent and solve problems involving addition and subtraction" (Cluster A) asks that students "Solve word problems that call for addition of three whole numbers whose sum is less than or equal to 20, e.g., by using objects, drawings, and equations with a symbol for the unknown number to represent the problem."

This part of the guide contains one chapter focused on each of the five domains for lower elementary school mathematics. At the beginning of these chapters, you will find a chart that provides an overview of that domain's clusters and standards by grade level. As in Part I's look at the ELA/literacy standards, here in Part II we will be referencing the content standards using a slightly abbreviated version of the CCSSI's official identification system. Again, we have dropped the first part of the code, the formal prefix ("CCSS.Math.Content"). The next piece of the code for standards in grades K–8 is the specific grade level, which is followed by the domain abbreviation, the letter identifying the particular cluster within the domain, and then the specific standard number. For example, "K.G.A.3" is shorthand for kindergarten, Geometry (the domain name), Cluster A (of the domain's two clusters, identified A–B), Standard 3.

Taken as a whole, the Common Core's mathematical content standards for the primary grades identify what students in grades K–2 should know and be able to do in order to establish the foundation for mathematics study over the course of their schooling. It is the nature of mathematics to build on concepts throughout the grades. The foundational addition concepts learned in 1st grade, for example, will allow students to understand multiplication in 3rd grade, and that understanding will allow students to understand algebraic concepts in middle school and high school, which will help prepare them for college and career. The developing conceptual understandings and procedural fluencies in these lower grades are essential for student success throughout their mathematics education.

The Standards for Mathematical Practice

Emphasis on students' conceptual understanding of mathematics is an aspect of the Common Core standards that sets them apart from many state standards. The eight Standards for Mathematical Practice, listed in Figure 7.2 and consistent throughout grades K–12, play an important role in ensuring that students are engaged in the actual use of mathematics, not just in the acquisition of knowledge about the discipline. Indeed, the table of contents in the standards document gives equal weight to the Standards for Mathematical Practice and to the Standards for Mathematical Content. This dual focus, echoed throughout the document's introductory material, has been undertaken to ensure the standards "describe varieties of expertise that mathematics educators at all levels should seek to develop in their students" (CCSSI, 2010g, p. 6).

The writers of the Common Core describe these practice standards in an introduction, explaining that the standards are derived from the process standards of the National Council of Teachers of Mathematics (NCTM) and the strands of mathematical proficiency found in the National Research

Council report *Adding It Up* (2001). A brief description of the meaning of the practice standards is provided in the front of the mathematical standards document (CCSSI, 2010g, pp. 6–8).

Figure 7.2 | **The Standards for Mathematical Practice**

MP1. Make sense of problems and persevere in solving them.

MP2. Reason abstractly and quantitatively.

MP3. Construct viable arguments and critique the reasoning of others.

MP4. Model with mathematics.

MP5. Use appropriate tools strategically.

MP6. Attend to precision.

MP7. Look for and make use of structure.

MP8. Look for and express regularity in repeated reasoning.

In addition to stressing mathematics proficiencies that cross all domains, the mathematical practice standards ensure that students who are focused on skills and processes don't find themselves engaged in rote activities that provide them no deeper sense of how mathematics works as an integrated whole. For example, adding and subtracting multi-digit numbers can be seen as a simple algorithm. In the past, standards documents required nothing more than that the algorithm be taught, which meant that often students were shown processes and expected to memorize them, without gaining a deeper understanding of the reasoning and meaning behind the algorithms. In contrast, the Common Core standards require that students use strategies based on place value and explain their reasoning for the strategies in 1st and 2nd grades. Students who are able to articulate their reasoning may gain a deeper understanding of multi-digit addition and subtraction, allowing them to see the utility of the process over a wider range of problems. This understanding will also assist them as they learn the algorithms in 3rd grade (3.NBT.A.2).

Please note that, as with the content standards, the mathematical practice standards have official identifiers, which we have shortened in this guide's sample lessons. For example, we abbreviate Mathematical Practice Standard 1, officially "CCSS.Math.Practice.MP1," as "MP1."

Implications for Teaching and Learning

A recent survey of more than 13,000 K–12 math teachers and 600 district curriculum directors across 40 states shows that teachers are highly supportive of the Common Core standards. That's the good news. On the other hand, the same survey shows that an overwhelming majority (80%) mistakenly believe that the standards are "pretty much the same" as their former state standards, and only about 25 percent of respondents are willing to stop teaching a topic that they currently teach, even if the Common Core State Standards do not support teaching that topic in their current grade (Schmidt, 2012).

These findings suggest some damaging possible consequences. For example, if teachers don't recognize the Common Core standards' new focus on depth of understanding, they may attempt to teach a broad curriculum that doesn't give students the time they need to develop that deeper understanding. Furthermore, teachers' unwillingness to stop teaching familiar or favorite content that the standards do not require reinforces the possibility that, while students may be exposed to a wide variety of mathematical concepts, they will not reach the required level of mastery set for concepts that have been identified as critical.

We want to highlight a document that can provide significant support for teachers' instructional efforts: the *Progressions for the Common Core State Standards in Mathematics* (Common Core Standards Writing Team, 2011). Still in draft form at the time of this writing but available online, it details some useful strategies for teaching the grades K–2 mathematics standards, and we urge anyone interested in specific strategies and examples to read it.

In addition to looking to the *Progressions* document as we wrote the chapters here in Part II, we relied extensively on the research of Julie Sarama and Douglas H. Clements to inform our discussion of the early learning pathways for children. Educators interested in specifics of the research that informed our descriptions should read Sarama and Clements's (2009) meta-analysis *Early Childhood Mathematics Education Research: Learning Trajectories for Young Children.*

How to Begin Implementation

As noted, the writers of the Common Core have offered some ideas for how to get started planning instruction and teaching the mathematics standards, and here in this guide, we share our own best advice.

Focus on the mathematical practice standards

The Standards for Mathematical Practice are one of the potentially challenging aspects of Common Core implementation. As described on page 82, the mathematical practice standards are found in two places in the standards document: in the overall introduction and in the introduction to each grade level. The guidance found in the document's introduction provides valuable insight into each mathematical practice standard, and we recommend that teachers become extremely familiar with these descriptions and spend some time planning how to incorporate the practices into their units. In Chapters 8–12, we offer our own ideas about how teachers might integrate the mathematical practice standards with each of the domains in the mathematical content standards.

Focus on critical areas

By sharpening the focus of each grade on three to four critical areas identified by the Common Core writers, teachers can help students develop a deeper understanding of those concepts than previous sets of mathematics standards required or allowed. The outcome is stronger foundational knowledge.

Focus on connections

Remember that the Common Core mathematics standards are designed to be coherent within and across grades. In our upcoming discussion of each domain, we will clarify how the concepts found in the elementary school mathematics standards are organized across grades, underscoring that each standard is best understood not as new knowledge but as an extension of ideas presented in previous school years. We believe that the better teachers understand these progressions, the easier it will be for them to let go of content that is no longer a critical area or an area of support for their grade.

The Standards for Mathematical Practice provide further correspondence between the standards at the grade levels and within the various domains; we highlight these connections in the ensuing chapters. However, it is important to stress that what we present are only a few examples of such connections; we do not mean to suggest that no other connections can or should be made. We encourage teachers to build on the proposals here to strengthen their own practice and enhance their implementation of the Common Core standards.

* * *

Now that we've looked at the overall structure of the Common Core standards for mathematics in the primary grades, we will examine each domain, addressing the specific standards at grades K, 1, and 2.

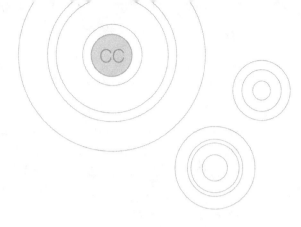

CHAPTER 8

Counting and Cardinality

The Counting and Cardinality domain (CC) is found only in kindergarten, and it contains content listed as critical in the standards' introduction to kindergarten. At this level, students are introduced to the concept of numbers, including written numbers, and what they represent. Figure 8.1 provides an overview of this domain.

Figure 8.1	**The Counting and Cardinality Domain: Grade K Overview**	
Grade Level	Clusters	Standards
Kindergarten	**K.CC.A** Know number names and the count sequence.	K.CC.A.1, K.CC.A.2, K.CC.A.3
	K.CC.B Count to tell the number of objects.	K.CC.B.4, K.CC.B.5
	K.CC.C Compare numbers.	K.CC.C.6, K.CC.C.7
Note: This domain concludes in kindergarten.		

In this chapter and the rest of the chapters here in Part II, we will first look at how the content of the domain relates to the Standards for

Mathematical Practice and then examine how the standards in each cluster relate to other mathematics content standards, both within and across grades. This close analysis is intended to clarify the meaning of every standard within the context of the entire set of Common Core mathematics standards.

Connections to the Standards for Mathematical Practice

The mathematical content and work with mathematical practices in kindergarten lay the foundation for mathematics in all subsequent grades. In particular, the Counting and Cardinality domain is the beginning of mathematical understanding—where students learn number names, the counting sequence, how to count objects, and how to compare numbers. The NCTM (2000) recommends that teachers support students' ability to make sense of numbers by creating classroom environments that promote the exploration of numbers, the development of conjecture, and dialogue about the thinking process. Early childhood researchers recommend play-based activities as a way to help younger students develop their abilities to make sense of problems and persevere in solving them, which is the focus of Mathematical Practice Standard 1 (Linder, Powers-Costello, & Stegelin, 2011). These researchers note that by doing this, teachers can help students develop their abilities to analyze situations and make sense of mathematics.

One way that kindergarten students learn how to "make sense" of mathematical situations is by using matching and counting strategies to compare the number of objects in two groups (CCSSI, 2010g). Teachers are encouraged to explore and develop these strategies by creating authentic problems for students to solve, such as figuring out if there are enough chairs in a circle for a group of students. A teacher might pose this problem and allow each group of students time to come up with an answer ("Yes, there are enough seats for everyone"/"No, there aren't enough seats for everyone") and to share how they did it (their strategy). Note that understanding and using simple matching and counting strategies help to develop students' problem-solving skills and make use of Mathematical Practice Standard 1.

As students count to answer "how many?" questions about objects arranged in different ways and represent a count of objects with a written numeral, they are learning that written numbers (abstract symbols) can represent situations in the real world. As they reverse the process—that is, given a number, they count out that number of objects—they are reinforcing this ability to reason both abstractly and contextually, a reasoning skill described in Mathematical Practice Standard 2. Once again, teachers can further students' reasoning skills by asking students to apply their counting and comparing skills to everyday problems that students encounter (e.g., having students count how many students there are at each table and then having students retrieve the correct number of rulers from a box of rulers so that there will be a ruler for each child at the table). This ability to apply familiar mathematical skills to everyday situations is an example of Mathematical Practice Standard 4, "Model with mathematics."

Kindergarten

The Common Core mathematics standards document identifies the use of numbers to represent quantities as a critical area for kindergarten. While geometric ideas are also identified as a critical area in kindergarten, an additional note in the introduction specifies that the majority of learning time in kindergarten should be "devoted to number" (CCSSI, 2010g, p. 9)—and, specifically, to representing, relating, and operating on numbers. As described in Chapter 7, educators are advised to focus their instructional efforts on the topics identified as critical areas for their grade level. Doing so helps to reduce the risk that they will take on too much content and be unable to implement the substantive changes the Common Core standards may require.

There are a total of seven Counting and Cardinality standards, organized into three topic clusters.

Know number names and the count sequence

Cluster A in the Counting and Cardinality domain focuses on number names and the count sequence (see Figure 8.2).

K.CC.A

Figure 8.2	**Know Number Names and the Count Sequence**

1. Count to 100 by ones and by tens.

2. Count forward beginning from a given number within the known sequence (instead of having to begin at 1).

3. Write numbers from 0 to 20. Represent a number of objects with a written numeral 0–20 (with 0 representing a count of no objects).

Research suggests that the ability to count using the number names and the correct count sequence is a skill that children develop over the course of several years (Baroody & Benson, 2001; Sarama & Clements, 2009). Sarama and Clements's *Early Childhood Mathematics Education Research: Learning Trajectories for Young Children* (2009) provides a guide to the progress that children may demonstrate in their early years, based on a number of research and standards documents. Using this guide, we can look at a typical pathway for students in relation to mastering number names and the count sequence.

Typically, students begin by being able to sing-song or chant number words from memory. As they grow a little older, they learn to verbally count with separate words but not necessarily in the correct order. Around age 4, children may be able to tell what number comes after a given number, but only after starting over at the number 1. Although children will come to school with a large variation in mathematical abilities, typically it is around kindergarten age (5 or so) that they begin to be able to count beyond 30 and to be able to count forward from a given number without having to go back to 1 (K.CC.A.2). Generally, the ability to skip-count by 10s to 100 is developed a little later, around age 6 (Sarama & Clements, 2009). Therefore, while the Common Core standards place counting to 100 by ones in the same standard (K.CC.A.1) as counting to 100 by tens, teachers may want to teach the two concepts at different times in the school year, depending on students' developmental pathways. The development of these basic counting skills and the ability to write numerals and grasp what numbers mean (K.CC.A.3) will be the basis for virtually all of the mathematics found in kindergarten (addition and subtraction, composing and decomposing numbers, and comparing measurable attributes). When they reach 1st grade, students will be asked to extend the counting sequence to 120 (1.NBT.A.1).

Count to tell the number of objects

While Cluster A focuses on students' ability to know the number names and sequence, the second cluster (Cluster B) focuses on counting objects (see Figure 8.3).

Figure 8.3 | **Count to Tell the Number of Objects**   K.CC.B

4. Understand the relationship between numbers and quantities; connect counting to cardinality.
   a. When counting objects, say the number names in the standard order, pairing each object with one and only one number name and each number name with one and only one object.
   b. Understand that the last number name said tells the number of objects counted. The number of objects is the same regardless of their arrangement or the order in which they were counted.
   c. Understand that each successive number name refers to a quantity that is one larger.
5. Count to answer "how many?" questions about as many as 20 things arranged in a line, a rectangular array, or a circle, or as many as 10 things in a scattered configuration; given a number from 1–20, count out that many objects.

Again, let's refer to Sarama and Clements's *Early Childhood Mathematics* (2009) to review the typical pathway for counting objects. Young children (around age 3) begin to count by pointing to objects, but they will often lose track of what they are counting. As they become more fluent in counting, they may develop the ability to keep one-to-one correspondence between counting words and a small number of objects laid out in a line. For example, when shown three apples on a table, a 3-year-old may be able to answer the question "How many apples are here?" by counting (or recounting) the apples ("One, two, three"). Around age 4, children can extend the count to give the number of objects and begin to understand that numbers tell how many. After counting small numbers, children this age learn to produce a certain amount of objects when asked, up to five objects. The Common Core standard K.CC.B.5 indicates that over the course of students' first year of school, the number of objects they are expected to count or produce will increase to 20. Early childhood research (Clements & Sarama, 2009) indicates that around the age of 5, students will have an explicit understanding of cardinality and will be able to count objects in different arrangements, as described in Common Core standard K.CC.B.4.

Compare numbers

Students will need to draw on their ability to understand what a number is representing in order to compare numbers—the focus of Cluster C (Figure 8.4).

K.CC.C

Figure 8.4 I **Compare Numbers**
6. Identify whether the number of objects in one group is greater than, less than, or equal to the number of objects in another group, e.g., by using matching and counting strategies. (Note: Include groups with up to ten objects.)
7. Compare two numbers between 1 and 10 presented as written numerals.

As Clements and Sarama (2009) note, children of 3 can be expected to be able to compare collections of objects that have a large discrepancy in size and know that one has more than another. By age 4, a child can be expected to recognize that different organizations of the same number are equal and different from other sets (e.g., if four balls are put into a row and then into two rows of two, a 4-year-old could be expected to identify the two sets of four as equal and as different from a set of three balls). Also by the age of 4, children can be expected to begin to compare small groups of objects (up to six) by using matching and counting strategies, though they may not always compare them accurately.

In the Common Core kindergarten standards, students are asked to use matching and counting strategies for groups of up to 10 objects (K.CC.C.6). This skill is typically considered to be a precursor to the next standard— comparing two written numbers (K.CC.C.7), a skill that research indicates is typically developed around the age of 6 (Sarama & Clements, 2009).

As previously noted, Counting and Cardinality is only found in kindergarten. However, the foundations laid here are critical for students' mastery of essential concepts, such as addition and subtraction. We will address these concepts in the next chapter, Operations and Algebraic Thinking.

CHAPTER 9

Operations and Algebraic Thinking

The Operations and Algebraic Thinking domain (OA) is found in the standards from kindergarten through 5th grade. Figure 9.1 shows an overview of the Operations and Algebraic Thinking domain for grades K–2.

Taken as a whole, the Operations and Algebraic Thinking domain in grades K–2 focuses on developing an understanding of and applying addition and subtraction. Our examination of this domain begins with a look at the associated Standards for Mathematical Practice.

Connections to the Standards for Mathematical Practice

Students will use several mathematical practice standards as they develop their understanding of addition and subtraction. As they gain familiarity with the operations, students will begin to use addition and subtraction to problem solve within real-world contexts, developed either by the teacher or by the students themselves. The National Council of Teachers of Mathematics cautions teachers not to underestimate the problem-solving capabilities of younger children and advises them to allow students the

Figure 9.1 ǀ **The Operations and Algebraic Thinking Domain:**
Grades K–2 Overview

Grade Level	Clusters	Standards
Kindergarten	**K.OA.A** Understand addition as putting together and adding to, and understand subtraction as taking apart and taking from.	K.OA.A.1, K.OA.A.2, K.OA.A.3, K.OA.A.4, K.OA.A.5
Grade 1	**1.OA.A** Represent and solve problems involving addition and subtraction.	1.OA.A.1, 1.OA.A.2
	1.OA.B Understand and apply properties of operations and the relationship between addition and subtraction.	1.OA.B.3, 1.OA.B.4
	1.OA.C Add and subtract within 20.	1.OA.C.5, 1.OA.C.6
	1.OA.D Work with addition and subtraction equations.	1.OA.D.7, 1.OA.D.8
Grade 2	**2.OA.A** Represent and solve problems involving addition and subtraction.	2.OA.A.1
	2.OA.B Add and subtract within 20.	2.OA.B.2
	2.OA.C Work with equal groups of objects to gain foundations for multiplication.	2.OA.C.3, 2.OA.C.4

opportunity to explore interesting, contextualized problems (NCTM, 2000). For example, teachers may wish to connect mathematics with science, asking each student to count the number of living things in a small section of a given area and to add up the totals with partners. This type of problem solving will allow students an opportunity to practice skills described by

Mathematical Practice Standard 1—"making sense of problems and perse-vere in solving them," as well as "modeling with mathematics" (Mathemati-cal Practice Standard 4).

As students in grades K–2 solve problems, they will be called upon to explain how they arrived at a given answer. As they explain their thinking about the problem, students can be encouraged to make conjectures, and teachers can assist them as they develop a logical progression of state-ments that explains those conjectures—skills related to Mathematical Prac-tice Standard 3 ("Construct viable arguments and critique the reasoning of others"). In addition, as students explain their mathematical reasoning, they should be encouraged to communicate using mathematical terms and to express their answers fully. This will help students to develop their abil-ity to communicate precisely—a focus of Mathematical Practice Standard 6, "Attend to precision."

Students in grades K–2 are beginning to see the structure and patterns found in addition and subtraction problems. For example, as they learn to "make 10" as a strategy for adding, they can begin to see and make use of the patterns found in the base ten number system. Students' understanding of these patterns employs Mathematical Practice Standard 7, "Look for and make use of structure."

Now that we've taken a high-level look at the domain as a whole, we'll explore the clusters found within each grade level and examine the stan-dards they contain.

Kindergarten

The Common Core mathematics standards document (CCSSI, 2010g) iden-tifies using numbers to solve quantitative problems as a critical area in kindergarten. Critical areas provide educators with a place to focus their efforts, minimizing the risk of taking on too much and therefore not being able to implement the substantive changes that the Common Core stan-dards may require. As noted in Chapter 8 (Counting and Cardinality), the introduction to the kindergarten standards states that more learning time in kindergarten should be devoted to representing, relating, and operating on numbers than to any other mathematics topic.

At the kindergarten level, the Operations and Algebraic Thinking domain contains five standards in a single cluster.

Understand addition as putting together and adding to, and understand subtraction as taking apart and taking from

In kindergarten, students are introduced to the concepts of addition and subtraction (see Figure 9.2).

Figure 9.2 | **Understand Addition as Putting Together and Adding to, and Understand Subtraction as Taking Apart and Taking From**

K.OA.A

1. Represent addition and subtraction with objects, fingers, mental images, draw-ings, sounds (e.g., claps), acting out situations, verbal explanations, expressions, or equations. (Note: Drawings need not show details, but should show the math-ematics in the problem. This applies wherever drawings are mentioned in the Standards.)

2. Solve addition and subtraction word problems, and add and subtract within 10, e.g., by using objects or drawings to represent the problem.

3. Decompose numbers less than or equal to 10 into pairs in more than one way, e.g., by using objects or drawings, and record each decomposition by a drawing or equation (e.g., $5 = 2 + 3$ and $5 = 4 + 1$).

4. For any number from 1 to 9, find the number that makes 10 when added to the given number, e.g., by using objects or drawings, and record the answer with a drawing or equation.

5. Fluently add and subtract within 5.

Research suggests that being able to understand mathematical opera-tions is a skill that children develop over the course of several years (Baroody & Benson, 2001; Sarama & Clements, 2009). According to Sarama and Clements (2009), it is around age 3 that a child typically shows the first signs of being able to reason about the effects of taking away or adding to a very small collection of objects and demonstrating a basic understanding of the concepts of "more than" and "less than." For example, if shown two separate small collections of objects (e.g., a set of two blocks and a third block in a different container), a 3-year-old may be able to pick out a number of objects that match the total (e.g., make a set of three blocks to match the total of the first two sets). Typically, around the age of 4 children are able to demonstrate comprehension of basic addition by verbally counting out a set of objects or fingers up to 5.

For an example of a kindergarten lesson addressing K.OA.A.3, please see **Sample Lesson 4.**

Here in kindergarten, children are asked to become fluent with adding and subtracting up to 5 (K.OA.A.5) and to be able to use objects, fingers, or drawings to add and subtract up to 10 (K.OA.A.2). These skills are directly related to the counting and comparing skills described in the Counting and Cardinality domain. In particular, students' ability to recognize that each successive number name refers to a quantity that is one larger (K.CC.B.4c) and to count to answer "how many?" questions (K.CC.B.5) will assist them as they solve addition and subtraction problems. There is a further cross-domain connection to the kindergarten standards within the Number and Operations in Base Ten domain, as the decomposition of numbers less than 10 (K.OA.A.3) can be considered a prerequisite to composing and decomposing numbers from 11 to 19 (K.NBT.A.1). While the Common Core standards do not explicitly state that one standard or cluster should be taught prior to another, the logical organization of ideas just described here indicates that there is such a sequence (learning number names and count sequence, counting to tell the number of objects, understanding addition and subtraction, and finally, composing and decomposing numbers), and it should be of special interest to those developing curriculum guides.

The second standard in this cluster (K.OA.A.2) asks students to solve addition and subtraction word problems. While the standard does not explicitly state what types of word problems should be used in kindergarten, the cluster heading specifies problems focused on *putting together and adding to* and *taking apart and taking from*. A brief description of these problem types, along with examples, is presented in Figure 9.3.

Figure 9.3 | **Addition and Subtraction Situations for Word Problems: Kindergarten**

Problem Type	Solve for	Example	As Equation
Add to (join; change plus situations)—a set of objects is presented, and more of those objects are added to that set (Start + Change = Result)	Result	There are three crayons on the table, and four more crayons are put on the table. How many crayons are on the table?	3 + 4 = ?
Take from (separate)—a set of objects is reduced by a given number (Start − Change = Result)	Result	There were six crayons in the box. Four crayons were taken out. How many crayons are left in the box?	6 − 4 = ?
Put together/Take apart (part-part-whole)—the set of objects presented is composed of different types of objects	Whole (total)	There are three girls and four boys sitting around a table. How many children are sitting around the table?	3 + 4 = ?
(First Part + Second Part = Whole)	Both Parts (both addends)	There are four chairs around a table. How many boys and how many girls can sit around the table?	? + ? = 4 4 + 0 = 4 3 + 1 = 4 2 + 2 = 4 1 + 3 = 4 0 + 4 = 4

Sources: CCSSI, 2010g (p. 88); Common Core Standards Writing Team, 2011; and Sarama & Clements, 2009 (p. 107).

Standards about fluency with numbers within 10 were not unusual in previous state standards. The fourth standard in this cluster (K.OA.A.4) follows this pattern to some degree, in that it asks for fluency with addition, but it differs by asking students to find the number that, when added to any number from 1 to 9, makes 10. This skill is a useful tool to have when learning how to add larger numbers, and it may help students develop strategies for addition. For example, when asked to add 6 + 7, a student who knows that 6 + 4 makes 10 may be able to decompose the numbers in the equation to make an easier problem: $6 + 7 = 6 + (4 + 3) = (6 + 4) + 3 = 10 + 3 = 13$. In 1st grade, students will build on this skill when adding numbers within 20 (1.OA.C.6).

The first, third, and fourth standards in this domain (K.OA.A.1, K.OA.A.3, and K.OA.A.4) state that students should represent and record addition and subtraction problems using equations. However, the introduction to the kindergarten standards makes clear that while kindergarteners should see addition and subtraction equations and be encouraged to write these kinds of equations, they should not be *required* to write equations in kindergarten (CCSSI, 2010g, p. 9).

Grade 1

The Common Core mathematics standards document identifies the development of strategies for adding and subtracting whole numbers as a critical area in 1st grade. Again, as described in the introduction to kindergarten, critical areas help identify a place for teachers to focus their efforts.

At the 1st grade level, the Operations and Algebraic Thinking domain contains eight standards grouped in four clusters.

Represent and solve problems involving addition and subtraction

The Common Core standards often follow a distinctive pattern across three grade levels when addressing a given concept. Typically, the standards introduce a topic (often informally) in one grade and then develop that topic further in the grade that follows, asking students to use strategies and properties to solve problems. In the third year of working with the concept, students are expected to develop fluency, or mastery, in the concept. This approach, which the Common Core takes toward addition and subtraction in grades K–2, allows for an extended focus on skills and concepts, providing students time to develop a deep understanding. Here in grade 1, Cluster A of the Operations and Algebraic Thinking domain (see Figure 9.4) focuses on developing students' understanding of the addition and subtraction concepts first introduced in kindergarten.

Figure 9.4 | **Represent and Solve Problems Involving Addition and Subtraction**
1. Use addition and subtraction within 20 to solve word problems involving situations of adding to, taking from, putting together, taking apart, and comparing, with unknowns in all positions, e.g., by using objects, drawings, and equations with a symbol for the unknown number to represent the problem.*
2. Solve word problems that call for addition of three whole numbers whose sum is less than or equal to 20, e.g., by using objects, drawings, and equations with a symbol for the unknown number to represent the problem.
*See Figure 9.5 for examples of these problem types.

Kindergarten students are asked to solve addition and subtraction word problems within 10 using visual and concrete tools (e.g., objects, fingers, or drawings) and to fluently add and subtract within 5 (K.OA.A.2). First graders build on and extend that earlier work, using addition and subtraction within 20 and addition of up to three whole numbers (1.OA.A.1–2) to solve word problems of the type illustrated in Figure 9.5.

Students in 1st grade are learning to represent addition and subtraction problems using equations with a symbol (e.g., a question mark, a box, a line, or a picture) to represent the unknown number in all positions (see Figure 9.5). Being able to use symbols for the unknown will ultimately allow students to use variables in mathematical expressions (as well as in equations and inequalities) in later grades. The abilities developed now, at these early stages of mathematics instruction, support later work evaluating expressions and generating equivalent expressions—skills that one day will help students succeed in algebra.

As mentioned, the common addition and subtraction situations shown in Figure 9.5 reflect the types of word problems that 1st grade students are expected to encounter in class. This figure is a compilation of information found in *Early Childhood Mathematics Education Research* (Sarama & Clements, 2009), the glossary of the Common Core standards document (CCSSI, 2010g), and the draft *Progressions* document (Common Core Standards

Figure 9.5 | **Addition and Subtraction Situations for Word Problems: Grade 1**

Problem Type	Solve for	Example	As Equation
Add to (join; change plus situations)—a set of objects is presented, and more of those objects are added to that set (Start + Change = Result)	Start	There were some crayons on the table. Three more crayons were placed on the table. Now there are five crayons on the table. How many crayons were on the table to start with?	$? + 3 = 5$
	Change	There were two crayons on the table. Some more crayons were put on the table. Now there are five crayons on the table. How many crayons were put on the table?	$2 + ? = 5$
	Result	There are two crayons on the table, and three more crayons are put on the table. How many crayons are on the table?	$2 + 3 = ?$
Take from (separate)—a set of objects is reduced by a given number (Start – Change = Result)	Start	There were some crayons in the box. Two crayons were taken out. There were four crayons left in the box. How many crayons were in the box before?	$? - 2 = 4$
	Change	There were six crayons in the box. Some crayons were taken out. There are two crayons left in the box. How many crayons were taken out?	$6 - ? = 2$
	Result	There were six crayons in the box. Four crayons were taken out. How many crayons are left in the box?	$6 - 4 = ?$

Figure 9.5 | **Addition and Subtraction Situations for Word Problems: Grade 1**			
Problem Type	Solve for	Example	As Equation
Put together/Take apart (part-part-whole)—there is one set, composed of different types of objects (First Part + Second Part = Whole)	First Part	There are seven children sitting around a table. Some are boys, and three are girls. How many boys are there?	? + 3 = 7
	Second Part	There are seven children sitting around a table. Four are boys, and some are girls. How many girls are there?	4 + ? = 7
	Whole (total)	There are three girls and four boys sitting around a table. How many children are sitting around the table?	3 + 4 = ?
	Both Parts (both addends)	There are four chairs around a table. How many boys and how many girls can sit around the table?	? + ? = 4 4 + 0 = 4 3 + 1 = 4 2 + 2 = 4 1 + 3 = 4 0 + 4 = 4
Compare—there are two sets of objects; the number of objects in each set is compared (Bigger Unknown – Smaller Unknown = Difference)	Smaller unknown ("X fewer")	Juanita has four more marbles than Ken. Juanita has seven marbles. How many marbles does Ken have?	? + 4 = 7 7 – 4 = ?
	Bigger unknown ("X more")	Juanita has four more marbles than Ken. Ken has three marbles. How many marbles does Juanita have?	4 + 3 = ?
	Bigger unknown ("X fewer")	Ken has four fewer marbles than Juanita. Ken has three marbles. How many marbles does Juanita have?	3 + 4 = ?

(continued)

Figure 9.5 | **Addition and Subtraction Situations for Word Problems: Grade 1 (*continued*)**

Problem Type	Solve for	Example	As Equation
Compare—there are two sets of objects; the number of objects in each set is compared (Bigger Unknown – Smaller Unknown = Difference)	Difference ("How many more?")	Juanita has seven marbles in her box. Ken has three marbles in his box. How many more marbles does Juanita have than Ken?	7 – 3 = ?
	Difference ("How many fewer?")	Juanita has seven marbles in her box. Ken has three marbles in his box. How many fewer marbles does Ken have than Juanita?	3 + ? = 7 ? – 4 = D

Sources: CCSSI, 2010g (p. 88); Common Core Standards Writing Team, 2011; and Sarama & Clements, 2009 (p. 107).

Writing Team, 2011). In the Sarama and Clements text, the authors explain that the types of addition and subtraction problems described in this figure have varying levels of difficulty. The easiest for students to solve are problems in which the results are unknown; the most difficult ones are those in which the start is unknown. Sarama and Clements suggest the difference in difficulty may be related to how easy it is for students to act out—or model—the problem with fingers or manipulatives. The draft *Progressions* document seems to concur with this assessment of difficulty, suggesting that while students in 1st grade should work with all of the types of problems found in Figure 9.5, they need master only the following types for problems within 20: *add to/take from* (solving for change), *put together/ take apart* (solving for either addend), and *compare* (solving for the smaller unknown, the "X more" version of the bigger unknown, and the "how many more?" version of the difference). This suggested progression appears to reflect the increase in difficulty of the three types of addition and subtraction situations.

Research indicates that another reason that these problems may be difficult for primary-grade students is that the semantics and vocabulary are somewhat complex (National Research Council, 2009; Sarama & Clements, 2009). Young children often struggle to distinguish similar words, such as *different* and *difference*, and this difficulty can lead to confusion when they are reading or listening to a problem. By asking students to articulate their thought processes, teachers may be able to identify and correct misconceptions related to vocabulary.

Asking students to articulate their problem-solving process has other instructional benefits, one of which is exposing students who are listening in to the idea that there are many different ways to solve problems. Research into early childhood mathematics tells us that connecting different solution methods developed by their peers can help students learn about the coherence of mathematics and support greater flexibility of thought in later grades (Sarama & Clements, 2009). In addition, and as noted earlier in this chapter, by presenting their solution methods, students will be practicing the construction of viable arguments and critiquing the reasoning of others—Mathematical Practice Standard 3.

Finally, the *Principles and Standards for School Mathematics* reminds us that some students in a 1st grade classroom will be able to solve addition and subtraction problems without referring to visual or concrete tools (e.g., blocks, their fingers), while others in the same classroom will still need the scaffold that such objects provide (NCTM, 2000). Research into the use of manipulatives and finger counting in younger children suggests that rather than slowing children down or interfering with their understanding, these methods are useful strategies for making sense of mathematics (Sarama & Clements, 2009). The same research indicates that students who are the most successful with manipulative and finger methods are the least likely to rely on these techniques long term. Because they feel more confidence in their solutions, they are able to progress more quickly toward faster, more efficient addition and subtraction strategies.

Understand and apply properties of operations and the relationship between addition and subtraction

Cluster B of the operations standards for 1st grade describes strategies for solving addition and subtraction problems (see Figure 9.6).

1.OA.B

Figure 9.6 | **Understand and Apply Properties of Operations
and the Relationship Between Addition and Subtraction**

---

3. Apply properties of operations as strategies to add and subtract. *Examples: If 8 + 3 = 11 is known, then 3 + 8 = 11 is also known. (Commutative property of addition.) To add 2 + 6 + 4, the second two numbers can be added to make a ten, so 2 + 6 + 4 = 2 + 10 = 12. (Associative property of addition.) (Note:* Students need not use the formal terms for these properties.)

4. Understand subtraction as an unknown-addend problem. For example, subtract 10 − 8 by finding the number that makes 10 when added to 8.

As is typical of the Common Core, the standards in this cluster emphasize a deep understanding of the properties of operations and the relationship between addition and subtraction. Students' understanding of these concepts builds a foundation that will support learning throughout the later grades as they extend their operational understandings to include multiplication and division (3.OA, 4.OA) and, eventually, to algebraic expressions in middle school (6.EE).

Add and subtract within 20

The concepts described in Cluster B will also help students as they use the strategies to add and subtract that are described in Cluster C (see Figure 9.7).

The Common Core's focus on the development of computation skill follows the distinctive, three-grade pattern we discussed earlier: introduction, extension, and then application. In kindergarten, students are asked to represent addition and subtraction with visual and concrete tools (e.g., objects, fingers, or drawings), to learn what numbers from 1 to 9 make 10, to decompose numbers less than or equal to 10, and to fluently add and subtract within 5 (K.OA.A.3–5). This introduces the concepts that will be more formally developed in the later grades. Here in 1st grade, students build on and extend that kindergarten work, adding and subtracting within 20 using strategies dependent on making 10 and decomposing numbers, and demonstrating fluency with addition and subtraction within 10 (1.OA.C.6). When students reach 2nd grade, they will be expected to use the mental strategies presented in this cluster to fluently add and subtract within 20 (2.OA.B.2).

1.OA.C

Figure 9.7 | **Add and Subtract Within 20**

5. Relate counting to addition and subtraction (e.g., by counting on 2 to add 2).

6. Add and subtract within 20, demonstrating fluency for addition and subtraction within 10. Use strategies such as counting on; making ten (e.g., $8 + 6 = 8 + 2 + 4 = 10 + 4 = 14$); decomposing a number leading to a ten (e.g., $13 - 4 = 13 - 3 - 1 = 10 - 1 = 9$); using the relationship between addition and subtraction (e.g., knowing that $8 + 4 = 12$, one knows $12 - 8 = 4$); and creating equivalent but easier or known sums (e.g., adding $6 + 7$ by creating the known equivalent $6 + 6 + 1 = 12 + 1 = 13$).

In kindergarten, students learned how to count forward from a given number in a count sequence (K.CC.A.2). The ability to count on without starting from 1 is noted as a "landmark" in children's numerical development (Sarama & Clements, 2009, p. 111), as it allows them to begin to add on objects without starting over from 1. The first standard in this cluster (1.OA.C.5) reflects this important achievement, asking that students use the counting-on strategy while adding. For example, when asked to add 3 and 2 together, a student might hold up three fingers; say, "Three"; and then hold up two more fingers and count out, "Four, five! The answer is five!" Sarama and Clements (2009) further note that children will often develop the strategy of counting on independently, after they have received concentrated instruction on addition. If students do not naturally develop this strategy on their own or after discussion with peers, development can be facilitated through direct instruction with no negative effects.

While the second standard in this cluster (1.OA.C.6) includes the counting-on strategy, it also emphasizes several other important strategies. As described in the *Principles and Standards for School Mathematics*, when teaching students addition and subtraction, it is important to allow students the opportunity to solve problems using different strategies and to discuss those strategies as a whole class (NCTM, 2000). By emphasizing the connections among the strategies, teachers will not only further students' understanding of these specific strategies but also deepen their understanding of mathematics as an integrated whole.

Work with addition and subtraction equations

The final cluster of operations standards for 1st grade furthers students' conceptual understanding of equations (see Figure 9.8).

1.OA.D

Figure 9.8	**Work with Addition and Subtraction Equations**

7. Understand the meaning of the equal sign, and determine if equations involving addition and subtraction are true or false. For example, which of the following equations are true and which are false? $6 = 6, 7 = 8 - 1, 5 + 2 = 2 + 5, 4 + 1 = 5 + 2$.

8. Determine the unknown whole number in an addition or subtraction equation relating three whole numbers. For example, determine the unknown number that makes the equation true in each of the equations $8 + ? = 11, 5 = \Box - 3, 6 + 6 = \Box$.

Several standards at earlier grade levels of the Operations and Algebraic Thinking domain ask students to use and understand equations (K.OA.A.1, K.OA.A.3–4, 1.OA.A.1–2). As is typical with the Common Core standards, however, the ultimate goal is conceptual mastery, not just being able to use equations. Here in Cluster D, 1st graders are asked to understand the meaning of the equal sign. This early understanding of what makes an equation true will help them understand later algebraic equations and concepts.

Note that the final standard in this cluster (1.OA.D.8) is very similar to the second standard in the domain's first cluster (1.OA.A.2), which asks students to solve word problems calling for the addition of three whole numbers using equations with a symbol for the unknown. Here, the standards' writers add some specificity to that earlier concept and extend it slightly by asking students to connect the idea of "true" equations to solving for an unknown number. Again, this understanding is likely to help students as they progress to solving more complex word problems and, later, when working with algebraic equations.

Grade 2

The Common Core standards identify developing fluency with addition and subtraction within 100, the focus of the Operations and Algebraic Thinking domain at this grade level, as a critical area in 2nd grade. In this section, we'll take a closer look at the three clusters and four standards found within the domain, starting with Cluster A.

Represent and solve problems involving addition and subtraction

The standards in Cluster A (see Figure 9.9) extend the concepts addressed in the 1st grade cluster of the same name as well as those addressed in the 1st grade Number and Operations in Base Ten domain (see Chapter 10).

Figure 9.9 | **Represent and Solve Problems Involving Addition and Subtraction**

2.OA.A

1. Use addition and subtraction within 100 to solve one- and two-step word problems involving situations of adding to, taking from, putting together, taking apart, and comparing, with unknowns in all positions, e.g., by using drawings and equations with a symbol for the unknown number to represent the problem.*

*See Figure 9.10 for examples of these problem types.

In 1st grade, students were asked to use addition and subtraction within 20 to solve word problems (1.OA.A.1) and to add within 100 using concrete models or drawings and strategies (1.NBT.C.4). Now, in 2nd grade, students extend this application to solving word problems within 100 and solving two-step problems. As described in our discussion of the 1st grade standards, when students reach 2nd grade, they are expected to master problems with unknowns in all positions (see Figure 9.10).

Figure 9.10 | **Addition and Subtraction Situations for Word Problems: Grade 2**

Problem Type	Solve for	Example	As Equation
Add to (join; change plus situations)—a set of objects is presented, and more of those objects are added to that set (Start + Change = Result)	**Start**	There were some crayons on the table. Three more crayons were placed on the table. Now there are five crayons on the table. How many crayons were on the table to start with?	? + 3 = 5
	Change	There were two crayons on the table. Some more crayons were put on the table. Now there are five crayons on the table. How many crayons were put on the table?	2 + ? = 5
	Result	There are two crayons on the table, and three more crayons are put on the table. How many crayons are on the table?	2 + 3 = ?

Note: In column 2, boldface text identifies problem types that students were introduced to in grade 1 and are expected to master in grade 2.

Figure 9.10 | **Addition and Subtraction Situations for Word Problems: Grade 2 (*continued*)**

Problem Type	Solve for	Example	As Equation
Take from (separate)—a set of objects is reduced by a given number (Start – Change = Result)	**Start**	There were some crayons in the box. Two crayons were taken out. There were four crayons left in the box. How many crayons were in the box before?	$? - 2 = 4$
	Change	There were six crayons in the box. Some crayons were taken out. There are two crayons left in the box. How many crayons were taken out?	$6 - ? = 2$
	Result	There were six crayons in the box. Four crayons were taken out. How many crayons are left in the box?	$6 - 4 = ?$
Put together/Take apart (part-part-whole)—there is one set, composed of different types of objects (First Part + Second Part = Whole)	First Part	There are seven children sitting around a table. Some are boys, and three are girls. How many boys are there?	$? + 3 = 7$
	Second Part	There are seven children sitting around a table. Four are boys, and some are girls. How many girls are there?	$4 + ? = 7$
	Whole (total)	There are three girls and four boys sitting around a table. How many children are sitting around the table?	$3 + 4 = ?$
	Both Parts	There are four chairs around a table. How many boys and how many girls can sit around the table?	$? + ? = 4$ $4 + 0 = 4$ $3 + 1 = 4$ $2 + 2 = 4$ $1 + 3 = 4$ $0 + 4 = 4$

(continued)

Figure 9.10 | **Addition and Subtraction Situations for Word Problems: Grade 2 (*continued*)**

Problem Type	Solve for	Example	As Equation
Compare—there are two sets of objects; the number of objects in each set is compared (Bigger Unknown – Smaller Unknown = Difference)	Smaller unknown ("X fewer")	Juanita has four more marbles than Ken. Juanita has seven marbles. How many marbles does Ken have?	? + 4 = 7 7 – 4 = ?
	Bigger unknown ("X more")	Juanita has four more marbles than Ken. Ken has three marbles. How many marbles does Juanita have?	4 + 3 = ?
	Bigger unknown ("X fewer")	Ken has four fewer marbles than Juanita. Ken has three marbles. How many marbles does Juanita have?	3 + 4 = ?
	Difference ("How many more?")	Juanita has seven marbles in her box. Ken has three marbles in his box. How many more marbles does Juanita have than Ken?	7 – 3 = ?
	Difference ("How many fewer?")	Juanita has seven marbles in her box. Ken has three marbles in his box. How many fewer marbles does Ken have than Juanita?	3 + ? = 7 ? – 4 = D

Sources: CCSSI, 2010g (p. 88); Common Core Standards Writing Team, 2011; and Sarama & Clements, 2009 (p. 107).

Add and subtract within 20

Cluster B in the Operations and Algebraic Thinking domain in 2nd grade (see Figure 9.11) contains one standard targeting fluency (being fast and accurate) with addition and subtraction within 20.

Figure 9.11 | **Add and Subtract Within 20**

2. Fluently add and subtract within 20 using mental strategies (*Note:* See standard 1.OA.6 for a list of mental strategies). By the end of Grade 2, know from memory all sums of two one-digit numbers.

As we mentioned when discussing the identically named "Add and subtract within 20" cluster for 1st grade (1.OA.C), the Common Core standards often follow a distinctive pattern of introduction, extension, and then application to develop a concept or skill over a span of three grade levels. Computing with addition and subtraction follows this pattern, beginning in kindergarten and ending here in 2nd grade with this standard (2.OA.B.2). In kindergarten, students are asked to represent addition and subtraction with visual and concrete tools (e.g., objects, fingers, or drawings), to learn what numbers from 1 to 9 make 10, to decompose numbers less than or equal to 10, and to fluently add and subtract within 5 (K.OA.A.3–5), introducing the concepts that will be more formally developed in the later grades. In 1st grade, students build on and extend their work from kindergarten, adding and subtracting within 20 using strategies dependent on making 10 and decomposing numbers, and demonstrating fluency with addition and subtraction within 10 (1.OA.C.6). Now, 2.OA.B.2 specifies that students be able to fluently add and subtract within 20 using the mental strategies listed in 1.OA.C.6, thus demonstrating mastery of those skills.

Work with equal groups of objects to gain foundations for multiplication

The strategies students have learned for adding and subtracting within 20 will help them as they begin to prepare for the 3rd grade concept of multiplication (see Figure 9.12).

In 2nd grade, we see the culmination of the topic pathway for addition (2.OA.C) and, with the informal introduction of multiplication, the beginning of a new topic pathway. This introduction is considered informal because the standards in Cluster C will simply lay the foundation for conceptual understanding of multiplication rather than present the topic. Students' official introduction to multiplication will come in 3rd grade (3.OA.A.1), and they will be expected to become fluent in the multiplication of single-digit whole numbers (3.OA.C.7). Then, in 4th grade, students will use their understanding of multiplication to find factor pairs and to multiply multi-digit numbers.

2.OA.C

Figure 9.12 | **Work with Equal Groups of Objects to Gain Foundations for Multiplication**

3. Determine whether a group of objects (up to 20) has an odd or even number of members, e.g., by pairing objects or counting them by 2s; write an equation to express an even number as a sum of two equal addends.

4. Use addition to find the total number of objects arranged in rectangular arrays with up to 5 rows and up to 5 columns; write an equation to express the total as a sum of equal addends.

Many of the skills associated with the ability to solve problems involving the four operations and the ability to discern and generate patterns addressed within the Operations and Algebraic Thinking domain are also addressed in other domains of the Common Core standards. As we will describe in the next chapter, the standards in the Number and Operations in Base Ten domain, which ask students to build and reason with the four operations, have a particularly close connection.

CHAPTER 10

Number and Operations in Base Ten

The Number and Operations in Base Ten domain (NBT) appears in the mathematics content standards for grades K–5. Here in the primary grades, this domain focuses on developing students' deep understanding of the base ten system and building their awareness of how the addition and subtraction of multi-digit numbers works.

Figure 10.1 provides an overview of the Number and Operations in Base Ten domain in grades K–2.

In this chapter, we'll first look at how the contents of the domain relate to the mathematical practice standards and then provide an overview of how each cluster relates to the other standards both within and across grades. This close analysis will offer a clearer understanding of the meaning of each standard within the context of the entirety of the Common Core standards for mathematics.

Taken as a whole, this domain focuses on the development and use of place value understanding, use of the properties of operations to extend the counting sequence, and performing addition and subtraction with multi-digit numbers. We will review each grade-level cluster individually and examine how its content connects and builds across the standards.

Figure 10.1 | **The Number and Operations in Base Ten Domain: Grades K–2 Overview**

Grade Level	Clusters	Standards
Kindergarten	**K.NBT.A** Work with numbers 11–19 to gain foundations for place value.	K.NBT.A.1
Grade 1	**1.NBT.A** Extend the counting sequence.	1.NBT.A.1
	1.NBT.B Understand place value.	1.NBT.B.2, 1.NBT.B.3
	1.NBT.C Use place value under-standing and properties of operations to add and subtract.	1.NBT.C.4, 1.NBT.C.5, 1.NBT.C.6
Grade 2	**2.NBT.A** Understand place value.	2.NBT.A.1, 2.NBT.A.2, 2.NBT.A.3, 2.NBT.A.4
	2.NBT.B Use place value under-standing and properties of operations to add and subtract.	2.NBT.B.5, 2.NBT.B.6, 2.NBT.B.7, 2.NBT.B.8, 2.NBT.B.9

Connections to the Standards for Mathematical Practice

As students learn about numbers and operations in base ten, they will also be engaging in several of the mathematical practices identified by the Common Core standards. In this domain, students will learn about place value and how to add and subtract numbers using strategies based on place value. To facilitate students' work with the strategies needed to solve these problems, teachers can spend classroom time discussing these problems, familiarizing students with other students' approaches to solving problems, and identifying correspondences and differences between different approaches. This problem-solving approach allows students to use the skills necessary to make sense of and persevere in solving problems—Mathematical Practice Standard 1.

As students illustrate and explain their calculations, including why the strategies that they used worked for them, they are developing their capacity to "construct viable arguments" (Mathematical Practice Standard 3) and "communicate precisely to others" (a skill related to Mathematical Practice Standard 6). As they construct these explanations, students will be selecting and using mathematical tools, such as concrete models or drawings, offering plentiful opportunities to "use appropriate tools strategically" (Mathematical Practice Standard 5). Students will also use Mathematical Practice Standard 7, "Look for and make use of structure," as they analyze the base ten number system and the properties of operations and use both to develop strategies to add and subtract multi-digit numbers. As they begin to generalize these strategies—grasp that a strategy developed for a specific problem can be used for other, similar, problems—and look for shortcuts, they will be using skills described by Mathematical Practice Standard 8—"Look for and express regularity in repeated reasoning."

Kindergarten

Although the content in the Number and Operations in Base Ten domain is not considered a critical area in kindergarten, and so should not be a major area of focus in this grade, it supports the critical content found in the Counting and Cardinality and Operations and Algebraic Thinking domains in kindergarten (see Chapters 8 and 9) and prepares students for the concept of place value, which is a critical area in 1st grade.

Work with numbers 11–19 to gain foundations for place value

At the kindergarten level, the Number and Operations in Base Ten domain has one cluster, containing just one standard (see Figure 10.2).

Although every child is different, research into early childhood education provides insight into children's typical developmental pathway for understanding mathematical concepts. Knowledge of these learning trajectories can support teachers' effectiveness in the classroom. In *Early Childhood Mathematics Education Research*, Sarama and Clements (2009) lay out the typical pathway students take when learning how to compose and decompose numbers using the base ten number system. Although children 2 years old and younger are typically able to "non-verbally recognize parts and wholes" of sets, they may not understand that groups can be composed of subgroups (p. 154). Between the ages of 3 and 4, children gain an intuitive grasp of the concept of commutativity and, later, of associativity. At this age, they may recognize that "a whole is bigger than its parts," but they cannot quantify with accuracy the number of objects in a set (p. 154). Between the ages of 4 and 5, children develop the capacity to grasp number combinations and to quickly name the parts of any whole, or the whole given the parts.

K.NBT.A

Figure 10.2 | **Work with Numbers 11–19 to Gain Foundations for Place Value**

1. Compose and decompose numbers from 11 to 19 into ten ones and some further ones, e.g., by using objects or drawings, and record each composition or decomposition by a drawing or equation (e.g., 18 = 10 + 8); understand that these numbers are composed of ten ones and one, two, three, four, five, six, seven, eight, or nine ones.

In kindergarten, the third standard within the Operations and Algebraic Thinking domain (K.OA.A.3) asks students to decompose numbers less than or equal to 10 into pairs in more than one way. The kindergarten standard within this domain, Number and Operations in Base Ten (K.NBT.A.1), also asks students to begin working with larger numbers, using objects or drawings to show how these larger numbers can be grouped into 10 ones plus some additional ones. For example, students might be given 16 blocks, scattered in a small area, and be asked to count them (a skill described by K.CC.B.5):

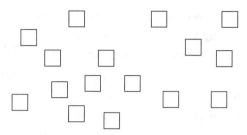

Students' next task would be to gather 10 blocks together, leaving 6 remaining:

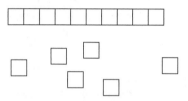

Although K.OA.A.3 specifies that students should "record each decomposition by a drawing or equation," the introduction to kindergarten in the standards document specifies that students at this level are to be encouraged to write equations but not *required* to do so. Students may be able to record this decomposition by writing the equation $16 = 10 + 6$ themselves, but if they cannot, a teacher may instead ask them to record the decomposition using drawings, for example, or by arranging pre-made cards that display numerals and symbols of operation:

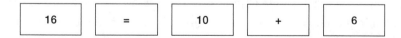

Practicing composing and decomposing numbers will help students when they reach 1st grade and are introduced to the idea of a tens place and a ones place in a two-digit number (1.NBT.B.2).

For more explicit descriptions of instructional strategies that are appropriate for teaching kindergarten students about the base ten system (e.g., number-bond diagramming, 5- and 10-frames, and place value layered cards), see the Common Core Standards Writing Team's draft *Progressions for the Common Core State Standards in Mathematics* (2011). Available online, the *Progressions* document also provides a short discussion of the common difficulties that children encounter because of the way that the English language structures number names, particularly numbers between 10 and 20. For example, although "15" can be read as "five ones and one ten" (*fif* meaning "five," and *teen* meaning "ten"), "25" is meant to be read in the reverse order—that is, as "two tens and five ones" (*twen* meaning "two," and *ty* meaning "tens"). This kind of information may further teachers' understanding of the intricacies involved in teaching this standard.

Grade 1

The Common Core standards document identifies extending the counting sequence, understanding place value for the tens and ones places, and using place value understanding to develop and use generalizable methods for addition within 100 and subtraction of multiples of 10 as critical content for the 1st grade. As noted, critical areas help teachers identify key content and provide a useful way for both teachers and students to take on new material that is significant but still manageable. In this section, we'll take a closer look at the Number and Operations in Base Ten domain at the 1st grade level, which contains six standards, grouped in three clusters.

Extend the counting sequence

The straightforward, single standard in Cluster A (see Figure 10.3) focuses on extending the counting sequence introduced in the kindergarten Counting and Cardinality domain.

In kindergarten, students are asked to count to 100 by ones and tens, and to write numbers from 0 to 20 (K.CC.A.1 and K.CC.A.3). When they reach 2nd grade, they will be asked to count, read, and write numbers within 1,000 and to skip-count by 5s, 10s, and 100s.

Figure 10.3	**Extend the Counting Sequence**
1. Count to 120, starting at any number less than 120. In this range, read and write numerals and represent a number of objects with a written numeral.

Understand place value

Next, let's look at Cluster B in the 1st grade Number and Operations in Base Ten domain (see Figure 10.4).

Figure 10.4	**Understand Place Value**

2. Understand that the two digits of a two-digit number represent amounts of tens and ones. Understand the following as special cases:
  a. 10 can be thought of as a bundle of ten ones—called a "ten."
  b. The numbers from 11 to 19 are composed of a ten and one, two, three, four, five, six, seven, eight, or nine ones.
  c. The numbers 10, 20, 30, 40, 50, 60, 70, 80, 90 refer to one, two, three, four, five, six, seven, eight, or nine tens (and 0 ones).
 	
3. Compare two two-digit numbers based on meanings of the tens and ones digits, recording the results of comparisons with the symbols >, =, and <.

As noted in the Operations and Algebraic Thinking chapter, the Common Core standards often follow a three-year pattern for developing a mathematical concept. They introduce a topic (often informally) in a lower grade, develop the topic further in the next grade, and ask for mastery of that concept in a third grade.

Students' beginning conception of the base ten system generally follows this pattern of introduction, extension, and application. In kindergarten, students were informally introduced to the base ten system, asked to compose and decompose numbers from 11 to 19 into 10 ones and some additional ones (K.NBT.A.1). The ability to perform these decompositions gives students a solid foundation for understanding base ten 1st grade concepts—that the number 10 can be thought of as a bundle of 10 ones, that the numbers 11 to 19 are composed of a 10 and a number of ones, and that numbers can be compared using the meaning of tens and ones digits (1.NBT.B.2, 1.NBT.B.3). This understanding will form the basis for students' future work with the base ten system, most immediately in 2nd grade, when they will begin to learn about the hundreds place.

Use place value understanding and properties of operations to add and subtract

Cluster C within this domain in 1st grade asks students to use what they know about the base ten system and about addition and subtraction to add and subtract numbers up to 100 (see Figure 10.5).

1.NBT.C

Figure 10.5 | **Use Place Value Understanding and Properties of Operations to Add and Subtract**

4. Add within 100, including adding a two-digit number and a one-digit number, and adding a two-digit number and a multiple of 10, using concrete models or drawings and strategies based on place value, properties of operations, and/or the relationship between addition and subtraction; relate the strategy to a written method and explain the reasoning used. Understand that in adding two-digit numbers, one adds tens and tens, ones and ones; and sometimes it is necessary to compose a ten.

5. Given a two-digit number, mentally find 10 more or 10 less than the number, without having to count; explain the reasoning used.

6. Subtract multiples of 10 in the range 10–90 from multiples of 10 in the range 10–90 (positive or zero differences), using concrete models or drawings and strategies based on place value, properties of operations, and/or the relationship between addition and subtraction; relate the strategy to a written method and explain the reasoning used.

Here, as in other places, the Common Core standards differentiate between strategies and algorithms. Algorithms, as defined by the writers in their *Progressions* document, are memorized sets of steps that rely on decomposing numbers and then performing operations with one-digit numbers (Common Core Standards Writing Team, 2011). The algorithm for multi-digit addition, for example, is to (1) add the ones column first to get a single-digit number, "carrying it over" to the tens place, if necessary; (2) add the digits in the tens place, plus the carried-over 10s; (3) repeat that for the hundreds place; and so on. A key feature of algorithms is that they are generalizable—applicable to all problems of a given type. In contrast, a strategy may be limited to a specific problem. It doesn't have to be efficient, and it may rely on drawings or manipulatives.

In 1st and 2nd grades, students are not expected to use algorithms. To be more exact, the Common Core expects these youngest students to develop and perfect their own strategies for addition and subtraction *before* they are introduced to standard algorithms. Here in the 1st grade, for example, the first standard in this cluster (1.NBT.C.4) expects students to develop strategies for addition and subtraction of a two-digit number (e.g., 26) and a single-digit number (e.g., 4) or a multiple of 10 (e.g., 30), using what they know about the base ten system and the properties of numbers and operations. If asked to add 26 + 30, for example, a student might use a set of blocks and begin by grouping blocks into bundles of 10:

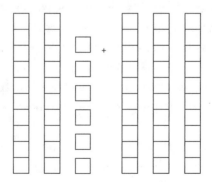

Once the blocks are laid out, the student might rearrange them to isolate the 10s and the 1s left over:

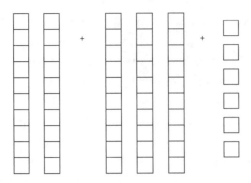

Finally, the student could link this addition strategy to a written method by recording an equation…

$$26 + 30 = 20 + 30 + 6 = 56$$

… and explaining his or her reasoning.

Standards 1.NBT.C.5 and 1.NBT.C.6 also require students to use models or drawings and strategies for adding 10 to two-digit numbers and for subtracting multiples of 10 from two-digit numbers. For additional examples of strategies for all standards in this cluster, please see the *Progressions for the Common Core State Standards in Mathematics* (Common Core Standards Writing Team, 2011). This experience with strategies promotes fluency with problem solving and the base ten number system and helps lay the foundation for work in 2nd grade, when students will be expected to become fluent with addition and subtraction within 100 and to begin to add and subtract within 1,000.

In addition to finding these connections across grades, we can also find connections between this domain and the other 1st grade domains, particularly Operations and Algebraic Thinking. Students' ability to add and subtract multi-digit numbers using the properties of operations is a clear extension of their ability to add and subtract single-digit numbers using the properties of operations—a concept that is developed in the Operations and Algebraic Thinking domain (1.OA.B).

Grade 2

The Common Core mathematics standards document identifies the extension of students' understanding of the base ten system (including skip counting, comparing numbers, and recognizing the meaning of the place value of digits up to the thousands place) as critical content for the 2nd grade. As noted previously, critical areas help educators focus their instructional efforts and prioritize the most important content. In this section, we'll take a closer look at the two clusters found within the domain and the nine standards they contain.

Understand place value

The first and fourth standards (2.NBT.A.1 and 2.NBT.A.4) in Cluster A (see Figure 10.6) focus on extending students' understanding of place value for whole numbers.

2.NBT.A

Figure 10.6 | **Understand Place Value**

1. Understand that the three digits of a three-digit number represent amounts of hundreds, tens, and ones; e.g., 706 equals 7 hundreds, 0 tens, and 6 ones. Understand the following as special cases:
   a. 100 can be thought of as a bundle of ten tens—called a "hundred."
   b. The numbers 100, 200, 300, 400, 500, 600, 700, 800, 900 refer to one, two, three, four, five, six, seven, eight, or nine hundreds (and 0 tens and 0 ones).

2. Count within 1000; skip-count by 5s, 10s, and 100s.

3. Read and write numbers to 1000 using base-ten numerals, number names, and expanded form.

4. Compare two three-digit numbers based on meanings of the hundreds, tens, and ones digits, using >, =, and < symbols to record the results of comparisons.

The concept of base ten was first introduced in kindergarten (K.NBT.A.1) and further developed in 1st grade, when students were asked to understand digits through the tens place (1.NBT.B.2). Now, in 2nd grade, students extend their understanding of the base ten system through the hundreds place, learning what the digits represent and using this understanding to compare numbers.

The second and third standards (2.NBT.A.2 and 2.NBT.A.3) in this cluster extend the counting sequence introduced in the kindergarten Counting and Cardinality domain. In kindergarten, students learn to count to 100 by 1s and 10s, and to write numbers from 0 to 20 (K.CC.A.1 and K.CC.A.3). In 1st grade, they learn to count, read, and write numbers up to 120. In 2nd grade, they must count, read, and write numbers up to 1,000 and skip-count by 5s, 10s, and 100s.

Use place value understanding and properties of operations to add and subtract

An understanding of place value, the focus of the standards in Cluster A, will help students add and subtract multi-digit numbers, the focus of the standards in Cluster B (see Figure 10.7).

2.NBT.B

Figure 10.7 | **Use Place Value Understanding and Properties of Operations to Add and Subtract**

5. Fluently add and subtract within 100 using strategies based on place value, properties of operations, and/or the relationship between addition and subtraction.

6. Add up to four two-digit numbers using strategies based on place value and properties of operations.

7. Add and subtract within 1000, using concrete models or drawings and strategies based on place value, properties of operations, and/or the relationship between addition and subtraction; relate the strategy to a written method. Understand that in adding or subtracting three-digit numbers, one adds or subtracts hundreds and hundreds, tens and tens, ones and ones; and sometimes it is necessary to compose or decompose tens or hundreds.

8. Mentally add 10 or 100 to a given number 100–900, and mentally subtract 10 or 100 from a given number 100–900.

9. Explain why addition and subtraction strategies work, using place value and the properties of operations. (*Note:* Explanations may be supported by drawings or objects.)

All standards within the K–2 clusters encourage students to develop and explain a wide variety of addition and subtraction strategies based on their understanding of place value and of the properties of operations (as described in the 1st grade standards 1.OA.B.3, 1.OA.B.4, 1.OA.C.5, and 1.OA.C.6).

The first two standards in this cluster (2.NBT.B.5 and 2.NBT.B.6) extend students' ability to add and subtract within 100. In 1st grade, students are asked to add within 100, including adding a two-digit number and a one-digit number or a multiple of 10 (1.NBT.C.4), and to add and subtract 10 more or 10 less of a number without having to count (1.NBT.C.5). Here in 2nd grade, students are asked to compute fluently, to subtract any two-digit numbers, and to add up to four two-digit numbers. All of these operations are to be carried out using strategies rather than algorithms, focusing on students' developing understanding of the base ten system and the properties of operations.

The third and fourth standards in Cluster B (2.NBT.B.7 and 2.NBT.B.8) build directly on the concepts of Cluster A regarding place value to the thousands place and extend students' ability to add and subtract with multi-digit numbers to include three-digit numbers. Again, students are asked to use concrete models or drawings and strategies based on place value rather than algorithms.

Although a focus on conceptual understanding and the ability to explain *why* a given strategy or algorithm works was unusual in previous state standards documents, this is often a focus of the Common Core standards. The final standard in this cluster (2.NBT.B.9) is a fairly typical example of such a focus, as it asks that students explain why addition and subtraction strategies work. These explanations need not be formal, and they may be supported with drawings or objects. In *Principles and Standards for School Mathematics*, the National Council of Teachers of Mathematics (2000) emphasizes that not only should students learn to explain their thinking but they should also have opportunities to listen to and reflect on the explanations of others. The teacher's role here is to support effective mathematical communication. When students have difficulty in understanding a peer's reasoning, for example, a teacher can guide that student to rephrase the explanations and to communicate more precisely and clearly.

As students develop fluency with the number system and with addition and subtraction within 100, they will begin to use these skills in a measurement context, as described in the next chapter.

CHAPTER 11

Measurement and Data

Throughout the elementary school grades, the standards in the Measurement and Data domain focus on developing conceptual understanding of data analysis and measurement, including length, time, and money. The Common Core takes an integrated approach to these concepts, drawing deliberate connections between measurement and data standards and content addressed in other domains. Rather than isolate the concept of picture and bar graphs, for example, the standards ask students to use these graphs to solve put-together and take-apart problems (see the discussion of Standard 2.MD.D.9, p. 141).

This integration of mathematical content was not common in prior state standards documents. The draft *Progressions for Common Core State Standards in Mathematics* (Common Core Standards Writing Team, 2011) explains that by providing context related to other domains, the standards not only help prepare students studying measurement and data analysis to learn statistics in later grades but also reinforce students' understanding of the operations they are studying now.

Figure 11.1 shows an overview of the Measurement and Data domain for grades K–2.

In this chapter, we'll review each cluster individually and examine how the content it addresses connects and builds across the standards.

	Figure 11.1 I **The Measurement and Data Domain: Grades K–2 Overview**	
Grade Level	Clusters	Standards
Kindergarten	**K.MD.A** Describe and compare measurable attributes.	K.MD.A.1, K.MD.A.2
	K.MD.B Classify objects and count the number of objects in categories.	K.MD.B.3
Grade 1	**1.MD.A** Measure lengths indirectly and by iterating length units.	1.MD.A.1, 1.MD.A.2
	1.MD.B Tell and write time.	1.MD.B.3
	1.MD.C Represent and interpret data.	1.MD.C.4
Grade 2	**2.MD.A** Measure and estimate lengths in standard units.	2.MD.A.1, 2.MD.A.2, 2.MD.A.3, 2.MD.A.4
	2.MD.B Relate addition and subtraction to length.	2.MD.B.5, 2.MD.B.6
	2.MD.C Work with time and money.	2.MD.C.7, 2.MD.C.8
	2.MD.D Represent and interpret data.	2.MD.D.9, 2.MD.D.10

Connections to the Standards for Mathematical Practice

Students will use several mathematical practice standards as they explore the concepts covered in the Measurement and Data domain and solve problems involving measurement and conversions of measurements and the representation and interpretation of data. To facilitate the deeper understanding of measurement and data analysis, teachers can assign problems that are practical and based in the real world. For example, students might be asked to develop a survey (with up to four categories) on a topic that interests them, develop a bar graph to capture survey responses, and then solve simple put-together and take-apart problems using their data and the data from another student. Teachers are further advised to spend class-room time discussing these problems, allowing students to consider their classmates' problem-solving approaches and prompting them to identify similarities and differences between their approaches and those of their peers. These strategies help students develop the skills necessary to make sense of and persevere in solving problems, as described in Mathematical Practice Standard 1. Sharing and discussing problem-solving approaches will also help students practice communicating their ideas with precision and clarity (Mathematical Practice Standard 6).

As students solve multi-step measurement and data problems in a con-text (whether real-world or mathematical), they need to be able to decon-textualize the problem—that is, restate it symbolically with numbers and know how to manipulate those numbers without thinking about the original context. Students' ability to make sense of and think through problems is enhanced when they are also able to contextualize—that is, see numbers as having a meaning in the context of a problem. The ability to reason abstractly (contextualize) and quantitatively (decontextualize) is described in Mathematical Practice Standard 2.

Students' capability to apply the concepts of measurement to problems arising in everyday life, society, and the workplace is related to Mathemati-cal Practice Standard 4, "Model with mathematics." As students learn about length, for example, they might be asked to apply the concept to real-world problems taken from science or posed by the teacher. They might also be asked to formulate problems that they find interesting and would simply like to be able to solve.

Finally, standards throughout this domain offer K–2 students multiple opportunities to "use appropriate tools strategically" (Mathematical Prac-tice Standard 5) as they learn how to use graphs to illustrate data as well as how to measure length and time.

Now that we've reviewed the Measurement and Data domain as a whole, let's explore the clusters and standards within the different grade levels.

Kindergarten

None of the measurement and data concepts addressed in kindergarten are listed as one of the Common Core's critical areas. Although measurement *is* identified as a critical area in 1st and 2nd grades, representing and interpreting data is not described as a critical area at any grade at the elementary school level. Thus, elementary school teachers may wish to view representing and interpreting data as content that supports the critical areas in other clusters and provides a foundation for the critical "statistical thinking" standards (6.SP.A) students will encounter in middle school mathematics. Although kindergarten teachers do need to address the standards described in this domain, these standards should not be a major focus.

At the kindergarten level of this domain, there are three standards, grouped into two clusters.

Describe and compare measurable attributes

The first cluster (Cluster A) introduces the idea of measurable attributes (see Figure 11.2).

K.MD.A

Figure 11.2 | **Describe and Compare Measurable Attributes**

1. Describe measurable attributes of objects, such as length or weight. Describe several measurable attributes of a single object.

2. Directly compare two objects with a measurable attribute in common, to see which object has "more of"/"less of" the attribute, and describe the difference. *For example, directly compare the heights of two children and describe one child as taller/shorter.*

Research suggests that being able to measure is a skill that children develop over the course of several years. Sarama and Clements's *Early*

Childhood Mathematics Education Research: Learning Trajectories for Young Children (2009) provides us with insight into the typical student pathway for understanding and using measurement.

Typically, at about the age of 3, children are able to identify length as an attribute, recognizing that things can be tall, short, big, or small. Here in kindergarten, the first standard in Cluster A (K.MD.A.1) asks that students identify physical attributes and be able to describe several measurable attributes of a single object. Teachers can facilitate this understanding by providing opportunities for students to practice this kind of observation. For example, a student looking at a rectangular block might describe it as "big." The teacher could follow up by asking which part of the block is longer and which part is shorter. (If students struggle with answering this question, the teacher can ask students to compare the sides of an identical block with the original.) The teacher might also ask students to pick up the block or even put it on scales to determine if the block is heavy or light. Kindergarten students can also learn about volume as a measurable attribute as they pour sand or water into containers of different sizes (NCTM, 2000).

The second standard in this cluster (K.MD.A.2) asks that students physically align two objects to determine which one is longer or whether the objects are the same length. This skill will assist students as they progress to 1st grade and are asked to measure lengths indirectly, using nonstandard units.

Classify objects and count the number of objects in each category

Cluster B introduces the concept of classification and categories (see Figure 11.3).

Figure 11.3 | **Classify Objects and Count the Number of Objects in Each Category**

3. Classify objects into given categories; count the numbers of objects in each category and sort the categories by count. (*Note:* Limit category counts to be less than or equal to 10.)

Sarama and Clements (2009) explain that there is little research available regarding early childhood acquisition of data analysis skills. Based on the learning pathway found in the standards, the single standard in this cluster (K.MD.B.3) is intended to prepare students to collect and organize data in later grades (1.MD.C.4, 2.MD.D). Note that by counting objects in various categories, students are reinforcing counting skills covered in the Counting and Cardinality domain (K.CC.B).

Grade 1

In 1st grade, students will build on the concepts of measurable attributes introduced in kindergarten and develop the abilities to measure length indirectly and to tell and write time. Understanding the meaning and processes of measurement, including iteration and transitivity, is a critical area in the 1st grade. As noted, critical areas provide educators with a place to focus their efforts, minimizing the risk of taking on too much and being unable to implement the substantive changes the Common Core standards may require.

At this grade level, the domain contains four standards in three clusters.

Measure lengths indirectly and by iterating length units

Cluster A focuses on students' ability to measure lengths (see Figure 11.4).

1.MD.A

Figure 11.4 | **Measure Lengths Indirectly and by Iterating Length Units**

1. Order three objects by length; compare the lengths of two objects indirectly by using a third object.

2. Express the length of an object as a whole number of length units, by laying multiple copies of a shorter object (the length unit) end to end; understand that the length measurement of an object is the number of same-size length units that span it with no gaps or overlaps. *Limit to contexts where the object being measured is spanned by a whole number of length units with no gaps or overlaps.*

Addressed in the first standard of this cluster (1.MD.A.1), the ability to understand transitivity (e.g., if object *x* is equal in length to object *y*, and object *y* is the same length as object *z*, then object *z* is the same length as object *x*) builds on students' experience in kindergarten describing and comparing measurable attributes (K.MD.A). According to *Early Childhood Mathematics Education Research*, understanding transitivity is key to understanding measurement, and the concept of transitivity may be dependent on students' understanding of conservation—that is, grasping that moving an object does not change its physical attributes (Sarama & Clements, 2009). Children typically develop both transitivity and conservation of constancy around age 4 or 5.

The second standard (1.MD.A.2) describes students' ability to tile the length of an object being measured, placing multiple copies of a shorter object along the length of a longer one with no gaps or overlaps, and count these iterations. Sarama and Clements (2009) point out that this ability is dependent on students' understanding of iteration (that is, that an object can be divided into equal parts). Many students in the 1st grade age range (ages 6–7) struggle with this concept initially, tending to view objects and numbers as a whole (e.g., they see 5 as a whole entity, not something composed of $1 + 1 + 1 + 1 + 1$). For this reason, in their book *Learning and Teaching Early Math* (Clements & Sarama, 2009), these researchers advise teachers to focus on helping students understand equal portioning and the transitivity principle (although students do not need to know these terms) rather than on the rote activity of using non-standard units to measure an object's length. Clements and Sarama also note that, while it is common for students to be asked to use several different types of measurement units in these early grades, research has shown that the use of different types of units when introducing the concept of iteration (*equal length* units) may confuse students. As they become more confident with the concept and recognize the need to use the *same* units when measuring an object, they will be able to use a wider variety of unit types. In 2nd grade, students will extend their understanding of length measurements to include the use of standard measurement tools—rulers, yardsticks, meter sticks, and measuring tape.

Tell and write time

Cluster B introduces the measurement of time (see Figure 11.5).

Figure 11.5 | **Tell and Write Time**

3. Tell and write time in hours and half-hours using analog and digital clocks.

The NCTM's *Principles and Standards for School Mathematics* (2000) notes that opportunities for teachers to talk about time occur often throughout the school day and can be naturally integrated into classroom activities. Teachers might create a daily schedule that includes pictures of clocks that children can compare to the actual clock and call attention to the time as the day progresses. In 2nd grade, students' ability to tell time will be extended to telling and writing time to the nearest five minutes.

Represent and interpret data

The third cluster in the 1st grade Measurement and Data domain (Cluster C) introduces the idea of data representation and interpretation (see Figure 11.6).

Figure 11.6 | **Represent and Interpret Data**

4. Organize, represent, and interpret data with up to three categories; ask and answer questions about the total number of data points, how many in each category, and how many more or less are in one category than in another.

The concept of data representation, presented informally in kindergarten with the classification and sorting of objects by count (K.MD.B.3), is formally introduced here in 1st grade. The single standard in this cluster (1.MD.C.4) asks students to organize and represent data with up to three categories and determine how many are in each category. These data may be generated from a teacher-led (e.g., science) investigation or from a student-led investigation.

The standard does not specify how the data should be displayed. The draft *Progressions for Common Core State Standards in Mathematics* document (Common Core Standards Writing Team, 2011) notes that students should be familiar with mark schemes, in which tally marks are used to represent individual data points; but otherwise, students and teachers are free to develop different ways to display data, and the *Progressions* document encourages a discussion about the relative strengths and weaknesses of each method. In 2nd grade, students will build on their abilities to represent data by using picture and bar graphs to represent a data set with up to four categories.

The content in 1.MD.C.4 also connects across domains, as it requires students to ask and answer questions about how many more or fewer data points are in one category as compared to another. By asking and answering these types of questions, students reinforce concepts developed in the Operations and Algebraic Thinking domain regarding the use of addition and subtraction to solve word problems (1.OA.A.1). This concept will be further developed in 2nd grade when students will be required to solve put-together, take-apart, and comparison problems with information found in a graph (2.MD.D.10).

Grade 2

In 2nd grade, students continue to work with measurement units and representing and interpreting data. Recognizing the need for standard units of measure is identified by the Common Core standards as a critical area in 2nd grade. As previously noted, critical areas provide educators with a place to focus their efforts, minimizing the risk of taking on too much and therefore being unable to implement the substantive changes that the Common Core standards may require.

As previously described in the kindergarten section of this chapter, data analysis is not considered a critical area anywhere within the elementary school grades. While it is content that is required by the Common Core standards, teachers may view it as supporting content for both the critical areas found in other clusters and the statistical thinking that will be addressed in later grades. Therefore, although the concepts found in the cluster regarding the representation and analysis of data (Cluster D) should be addressed, they should not be a primary focus in this grade.

At the 2nd grade level, the Measurement and Data domain contains 10 standards in four clusters.

Measure and estimate lengths in standard units

Figure 11.7 shows the standards found in Cluster A.

2.MD.A

Figure 11.7 | **Measure and Estimate Lengths in Standard Units**

1. Measure the length of an object by selecting and using appropriate tools such as rulers, yardsticks, meter sticks, and measuring tapes.

2. Measure the length of an object twice, using length units of different lengths for the two measurements; describe how the two measurements relate to the size of the unit chosen.

3. Estimate lengths using units of inches, feet, centimeters, and meters.

4. Measure to determine how much longer one object is than another, expressing the length difference in terms of a standard length unit.

In kindergarten, students are asked to describe measurable attributes and to directly compare two objects with a measureable attribute in common. Students in 1st grade begin to develop an understanding of iteration and transitivity—that an object can be divided into multiple equal parts and measured using a reference object. Here in 2nd grade, the standards in Cluster A extend those measurement concepts to include standard units.

The first standard in the cluster (2.MD.A.1) asks that students select and use appropriate measurement devices. The NCTM's *Principles and Standards for School Mathematics* (2000) recommends that students be given access to a number of different measurement tools with different types of units. As students work with different tools, they should come to recognize that different units provide different levels of precision, and different tools are useful for different circumstances. This understanding leads directly to the second standard in this cluster (2.MD.A.2), which asks that students describe how the size of the units can affect the reported measurement of an object. Recognizing that smaller units will require more iterations to cover a given length is a concept identified as critical by the Common Core standards.

As students become familiar with physical measurement, they build the readiness necessary to estimate measurements by mentally dividing objects into familiar units, the focus of the cluster's third standard (2.MD.A.3). The final standard in this cluster (2.MD.A.4) relates directly to the comparison skills described in the Operations and Algebraic Thinking domain (1.OA.A), asking students to express the length difference between two objects. Students will use this skill further in grade 3, as they begin to work with area and perimeter (3.MD.C).

Relate addition and subtraction to length

The next cluster links measurement and addition and subtraction (see Figure 11.8).

Figure 11.8	**Relate Addition and Subtraction to Length**

5. Use addition and subtraction within 100 to solve word problems involving lengths that are given in the same units, e.g., by using drawings (such as drawings of rulers) and equations with a symbol for the unknown number to represent the problem.

6. Represent whole numbers as lengths from 0 on a number line diagram with equally spaced points corresponding to the numbers 0, 1, 2, ..., and represent whole-number sums and differences within 100 on a number line diagram.

The explicit connection of measurement to addition and subtraction word problems found in the first standard of Cluster B (2.MD.B.5) is not typical in prior state standards documents, which often treated the two concepts separately. The deliberate connecting of these two concepts allows students to see mathematics as an integrated whole rather than a series of individual ideas and reinforces their understanding of both concepts.

The second standard (2.MD.B.6) marks students' first introduction to the concept of a number line. It connects the ideas of counting, addition and subtraction, and unit length. This concept will be further extended when students are asked to use a line plot to show data in both 2nd grade (see the discussion of Cluster D) and 3rd grade (3.MD.B.4).

Work with time and money

Cluster C in the 2nd grade Measurement and Data domain extends students' developing understanding of time and presents the standards' first focus on the concept of money (see Figure 11.9).

2.MD.C

Figure 11.9 | **Work with Time and Money**

7. Tell and write time from analog and digital clocks to the nearest five minutes, using a.m. and p.m.

8. Solve word problems involving dollar bills, quarters, dimes, nickels, and pennies, using $ and ¢ symbols appropriately. *Example: If you have 2 dimes and 3 pennies, how many cents do you have?*

In 1st grade, students are introduced to the concept of time and are asked to tell and write time to the nearest half hour (1.MD.B.3). Here in 2nd grade, the first standard in this cluster (2.MD.C.7) asks students to extend their skills to include telling and writing time to the nearest five minutes and using *a.m.* and *p.m.*

The second standard introduces the concept of money (2.MD.C.8). Money will be addressed again in 4th grade, when students will be asked to use the four operations to solve word problems involving money (4.MD.2).

Fourth grade also introduces decimal notation to the hundredths place, allowing students to express money problems with decimal notation.

Represent and interpret data

The final cluster in this domain (Cluster D) extends students' ability to represent and interpret data (see Figure 11.10).

Figure 11.10 | **Represent and Interpret Data**

2.MD.D

9. Generate measurement data by measuring lengths of several objects to the nearest whole unit, or by making repeated measurements of the same object. Show the measurements by making a line plot, where the horizontal scale is marked off in whole-number units.

10. Draw a picture graph and a bar graph (with single-unit scale) to represent a data set with up to four categories. Solve simple put-together, take-apart, and compare problems* using information presented in a bar graph.

*See Figure 9.10 on pp. 110–112 and Table 1 in the glossary of the mathematics standards document (CCSSI, 2010g, p. 88) for clarification of these problem types.

The content of the standards within this cluster has its roots in kindergarten, when students were asked to classify and sort objects. In 1st grade, students extended this ability to include data and learned to organize, represent, and interpret data with up to three categories. Here in 2nd grade, students will draw on the skills described in Cluster A (measuring lengths in standard units) to generate data and then record these data using a number line, a concept addressed in Cluster B.

For example, students might measure the lengths of several potted plants to the nearest centimeter. Then, with teacher guidance, they would create a number line to capture the appropriate range of length measurements and then indicate, with marks above the number line, the number of plants with the given measurements, like so:

For an example of a 2nd grade lesson addressing 2.MD.D.9, please see **Sample Lesson 6.**

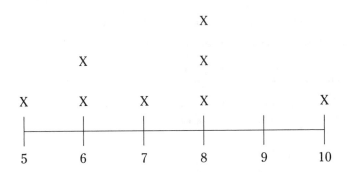

The ability to create this kind of simple line plot will assist students in 3rd grade, when they will be asked to create a line plot to include the 3rd grade concept of quarter and half units (3.MD.B.4).

The second standard in the cluster (2.MD.D.10) introduces the concept of picture and bar graphs. In 1st grade, students were asked to represent data in up to three categories (1.MD.C.4); however, that 1st grade standard did not specify how students were to represent those data. Here in 2nd grade, students are asked to use a specific representation (bar and picture graphs) to assist them as they solve problems. The problem types described in this standard are the same as those described by the first standard in the Operations and Algebraic Thinking domain (2.OA.A.1). Teachers might draw students' attention to this deliberate connection to stress the interconnected nature of mathematics.

As students begin to master their measurement and categorization skills, they will be able to utilize them as they practice geometry, as described in the next chapter.

CHAPTER 12

Geometry

In this chapter, we'll look at the Geometry domain (G), first reviewing how the contents of the domain relate to the Standards for Mathematical Practice and then providing an overview of how the content of each cluster relates to the other standards both within and across grades. This close analysis will clarify the meaning of each standard within the context of the entirety of the Common Core standards for mathematics, and it will also consider the research-indicated conceptual underpinnings for the standards.

Figure 12.1 provides an overview of the Geometry domain for grades K–2. Note that the sole cluster in both grades 1 and 2 seems to be a duplicate: "Reason with shapes and their attributes." Although we'll find that the content addressed in the two grades is slightly different, this repetition is unusual within the Common Core standards.

As a review of the clusters within this K–2 grade band makes clear, the Geometry domain focuses on two major aspects of geometry: understanding and reasoning with shapes and their properties, and the creation and composition of shapes.

Figure 12.1 | **The Geometry Domain: Grades K–2 Overview**

Grade Level	Clusters	Standards
Kindergarten	**K.G.A** Identify and describe shapes.	K.G.A.1, K.G.A.2, K.G.A.3
	K.G.B Analyze, compare, create, and compose shapes.	K.G.B.4, K.G.B.5, K.G.B.6
Grade 1	**1.G.A** Reason with shapes and their attributes.	1.G.A.1, 1.G.A.2, 1.G.A.3
Grade 2	**2.G.A** Reason with shapes and their attributes.	2.G.A.1, 2.G.A.2, 2.G.A.3

Connections to the Standards for Mathematical Practice

In conjunction with building their knowledge of geometric concepts, students in the early elementary grades will be developing and using several essential mathematical practices. As students become comfortable with composing shapes, they may be challenged to solve problems related to the composition of complex and three-dimensional shapes. For example, a teacher might challenge students to create and record all the shapes that it is possible to create with two triangles, or to make a block animal out of rectangular prisms (NCTM, 2000). While students perform these tasks, teachers can ask questions and offer encouragement that will keep students on track and support their ability to make sense of the problem. As they participate in these activities, students will engage in and begin to develop Mathematical Practice Standard 1—"Make sense of problems and persevere in solving them."

As they work, students can also be encouraged to develop their own questions and engage in discussions with their teachers and their peers. These discussions will help students to understand the approaches that other students may have taken and encourage further questions and dialogue. In addition, as part of these dialogues, teachers can encourage students to make conjectures about the geometric compositions (e.g., the number of different ways to make a rhombus, given certain shapes), test those conjectures, and then explain the testing method to other students. Constructing these explanations gives students an opportunity to use their geometric vocabulary, describing the shapes and their attributes with precision. With practice and assistance from the teacher, these types of dialogues can allow students to use skills associated with Mathematical Practice Standards 3 and 6: "Construct viable arguments" and "Attend to precision."

The National Council of Teachers of Mathematics encourages teachers to provide students with a variety of materials they can use to explore shapes, such as building blocks, household items (such as cereal boxes), geoboards, and interactive computer programs (NCTM, 2000). Access to these tools will allow students multiple opportunities to apply the geometric concepts that they know in everyday life (Mathematical Practice Standard 4) and to "use appropriate tools strategically" (Mathematical Practice Standard 5).

Kindergarten

One of the two critical areas identified for kindergarten by the Common Core standards document is the ability to describe the objects in the environment using geometric ideas and vocabulary (e.g., shape, orientation, spatial relations) and to correctly name and describe basic two- and three-dimensional shapes.

At the kindergarten level, the Geometry domain contains six standards in two clusters.

Identify and describe shapes (squares, circles, triangles, rectangles, hexagons, cubes, cones, cylinders, and spheres)

Cluster A introduces the idea of shape recognition (see Figure 12.2).

> Figure 12.2 | **Identify and Describe Shapes (Squares, Circles, Triangles, Rectangles, Hexagons, Cubes, Cones, Cylinders, and Spheres)**
>
> 1. Describe objects in the environment using names of shapes, and describe the relative positions of these objects using terms such as *above, below, beside, in front of, behind,* and *next to.*
>
> 2. Correctly name shapes regardless of their orientations or overall size.
>
> 3. Identify shapes as two-dimensional (lying in a plane, "flat") or three-dimensional ("solid").

According to research, the ability to recognize shapes is a skill that children develop over the course of several years. Sarama and Clements's *Early Childhood Mathematics Education Research: Learning Trajectories for Young Children* (2009) provides insight into the typical developmental pathway for a student learning about shapes. Typically, children first show signs of understanding what a shape is around age 2, when they are able to match basic shapes of the same size and orientation. Within the same year, they begin to be able to match shapes with different sizes and orientations (e.g., recognizing that a large circle is the same shape as a small circle). Around age 3, many children, given assistance, can recognize and name basic prototypical shapes (circles, squares, and sometimes triangles and rectangles) and match combinations of shapes to each other. For example, they may recognize that a given shape is a rectangle because it "looks like a door" (Sarama & Clements, 2009, p. 82). Typically it's around age 4 that children are able to recognize some nonprototypical squares and triangles; at age 5, the common age in kindergarten, they can usually recognize simple shapes (e.g., rectangles or triangles) regardless of their orientation or size, as described by standard K.G.A.2. Kindergarteners are also expected to be able to describe their world using the names of shapes and positional terms (K.G.A.1) and identify whether a shape is two- or three-dimensional (K.G.A.3).

Analyze, compare, create, and compose shapes

Cluster B deepens students' understanding of geometric ideas (see Figure 12.3).

K.G.B

Figure 12.3	**Analyze, Compare, Create, and Compose Shapes**
4. Analyze and compare two- and three-dimensional shapes, in different sizes and orientations, using informal language to describe their similarities, differences, parts (e.g., number of sides and vertices/"corners") and other attributes (e.g., having sides of equal length).
5. Model shapes in the world by building shapes from components (e.g., sticks and clay balls) and drawing shapes.
6. Compose simple shapes to form larger shapes. *For example, "Can you join these two triangles with full sides touching to make a rectangle?"*

Again, let's refer to Sarama and Clements (2009)—this time to review the pathway for comparing geometric shapes and composing geometric shapes, starting with the former.

Children typically generate the first sign of understanding how to compare geometric shapes around the age of 2, when they begin to compare real-world objects and explain if two things (such as houses) are the same or different, based on shape. At about 4 years old, a child can usually use objects (such as sticks) to create a shape such as a triangle; judge two shapes as the same if they are more visually similar than different (e.g., they both have a pointy top); and match shapes on one side by placing them next to or on top of each other. With this degree of readiness assumed, the Common Core asks kindergarten students to analyze and compare two- and three-dimensional shapes (K.G.B.4) by looking at the attributes of the shapes. Teachers should be aware that students' initial comparisons may be based on looking at some attributes of shapes but overlooking others. A student might, for example, identify two rectangles with equal width but unequal length as being the same size. A sign of development (typically evidenced around age 6) is when students asked to compare shapes will examine all attributes and spatial relationships.

Turning to the development pathway for composing geometric shapes, often the earliest sign that children are beginning to be able to manipulate shapes is demonstrated at age 2, when they start to manipulate individual shapes and decompose shapes through trial and error. For example, children may, through trial and error, re-create simple shape pictures using physical pattern blocks. At this simplest level, each shape in the picture should not only be outlined but also only touch at points so that the matching is as easy as possible. Around age 4, children can begin to make pictures by placing shapes into outlines that combine shapes by matching sides (Clements & Sarama, 2009). Here in kindergarten, students will be challenged to extend their ability to make pictures from outlines, as they are asked to make simple shapes to form larger shapes (K.G.B.6). A sign of development (again, typically demonstrated around age 6) appears when the student composes purposefully and deliberately rather than through trial and error, choosing angles and side lengths (Sarama & Clements, 2009).

This foundation in shapes will help students as they progress to 1st and 2nd grades and begin to look at how shapes are alike and different and learn that shapes can have a given number of angles or faces.

Grade 1

The Common Core standards document identifies the ability to compose and decompose plane and solid figures and an understanding of part–whole relationships and the properties of shapes as critical areas in 1st grade. This ability to "reason with shapes and their attributes" is the focus of the three standards of the 1st grade Geometry domain.

Reason with shapes and their attributes

Let's take a closer look at the 1st grade geometry standards, which are grouped in a single cluster (see Figure 12.4).

Figure 12.4 | **Reason with Shapes and Their Attributes**   **1.G.A**

1. Distinguish between defining attributes (e.g., triangles are closed and three-sided) versus non-defining attributes (e.g., color, orientation, overall size); build and draw shapes to possess defining attributes.

2. Compose two-dimensional shapes (rectangles, squares, trapezoids, triangles, half-circles, and quarter-circles) or three-dimensional shapes (cubes, right rectangular prisms, right circular cones, and right circular cylinders) to create a composite shape, and compose new shapes from the composite shape. (*Note:* Students do not need to learn formal names such as "right rectangular prism.")

3. Partition circles and rectangles into two and four equal shares, describe the shares using the words *halves*, *fourths*, and *quarters*, and use the phrases *half of*, *fourth of*, and *quarter of*. Describe the whole as two of, or four of the shares. Understand for these examples that decomposing into more equal shares creates smaller shares.

The ability to distinguish between defining and non-defining attributes (1.G.A.1) builds directly on the kindergarten content, extending students' ability to analyze and compare two- and three-dimensional shapes using informal language (K.G.B.4). In order to help students develop a deeper understanding of the attributes of shapes, teachers can use visual and kinesthetic exercises. For example, a teacher might use masking tape to create a shape (such as a triangle) on the floor and, as part of a game, challenge students to name an attribute of the shape (e.g., *Teacher:* "How do you know that's a triangle?" *Student:* "Because a triangle has three sides.") (Clements & Sarama, 2009).

The ability to compose two- and three-dimensional shapes, the focus of the second standard (1.G.A.2), also has its roots in skills learned earlier. In kindergarten, students are asked to compose simple shapes to make larger shapes (K.G.B.6). The ability to make new shapes out of composite shapes provides the foundation necessary for subsequent understanding. In the near future, it will help students to recognize and draw shapes with specific defining attributes (2.G.A.1); several years on, in

For an example of a 1st grade lesson addressing 1.G.A.2 and demonstrating one method of teaching the composition of two-dimensional shapes, please see **Sample Lesson 5.**

middle school, it will enable them to grasp the concepts of similarity and congruence (8.G.A).

The final geometry standard for first grade (1.G.A.3) informally introduces fractional concepts as equal shares of shapes and introduces the idea that the creation of more shares creates smaller shares. This groundwork will continue in 2nd grade, when students will be asked to partition circles and rectangles into thirds, halves, and fourths (2.G.A.3). Here in the primary grades, students are permitted to use a visual estimation of the size of the parts to help them judge if the shapes are equal. In later grades, they will be expected to use more precision, using measurement to judge if parts are equal.

The early and gradual introduction to fractions that the Common Core standards provide, presenting them as a geometric concept in grades 1 and 2 and then as a numeric concept in grade 3 (3.NF), fosters a deep conceptual understanding. It also connects the domains of Geometry and Number and Operations—Fractions, allowing for greater coherence within the standards.

Grade 2

The Common Core standards document identifies the ability to describe and analyze shapes as critical content for 2nd grade. Paralleling the 1st grade Geometry domain, 2nd grade Geometry also contains three standards in a single cluster.

Reason with shapes and their attributes

The geometric concepts addressed in the 2nd grade standards (see Figure 12.5) are small extensions of the concepts covered in the 1st grade Geometry domain.

In 1st grade, students were asked to distinguish between defining and non-defining attributes and to build and draw shapes to possess defining attributes (1.G.A.1). The first standard in 2nd grade Geometry (2.G.A.1) draws upon students' ability to draw shapes with defining attributes, asking them to draw shapes with a given number of angles or a given number of equal faces and to identify a number of two-dimensional shapes and cubes. This extends students' formal understanding of shapes and their attributes, which should help students in 3rd grade as they begin to classify shapes by their sides and angles (3.G.A.1), and lays the foundation for understanding similarity and congruence in later grades (8.G.A).

Figure 12.5 | **Reason with Shapes and Their Attributes**

2.G.A

1. Recognize and draw shapes having specified attributes, such as a given number of angles or a given number of equal faces. (*Note:* Sizes are compared directly or visually, not compared by measuring.) Identify triangles, quadrilaterals, pentagons, hexagons, and cubes.

2. Partition a rectangle into rows and columns of same-size squares and count to find the total number of them.

3. Partition circles and rectangles into two, three, or four equal shares, describe the shares using the words *halves*, *thirds*, *half of*, *a third of*, etc., and describe the whole as two halves, three thirds, four fourths. Recognize that equal shares of identical wholes need not have the same shape.

As described in previous chapters, the Common Core standards frequently introduce a topic informally in a lower grade, formally develop it in the next, and expect mastery in a third grade. Here in 2nd grade, the second standard in the Geometry domain (2.G.A.2), which builds on students' ability to partition shapes (1.G.A.3), serves as an informal introduction to the concept of area. In 3rd grade, students will begin to formally develop the concept of area as an attribute of plane figures and to measure areas by counting unit squares (3.MD.C). In 4th grade, they will be asked to apply the area formulas for rectangles in problem solving (4.MD.A.3). This gradual, three-stage approach allows teachers to teach concepts deeply and to make connections across the mathematical domains, such as connecting area (Geometry) to multiplication (Operations and Algebraic Thinking).

The final standard in the 2nd grade Geometry domain (2.G.A.3) extends students' ability to partition circles and rectangles. In 1st grade, students were asked to partition circles and rectangles into two and four equal shares (1.G.A.3). Here in 2nd grade, students learn to partition these shapes into three equal shares, using the term *thirds*. First grade students were asked to describe the whole as two or four of the shares; in 2nd grade, the connection to the fractional terms is extended with two halves, three thirds, and four fourths. Finally, students are asked to recognize that equal shares of identical wholes need not have the same shape—that is, that shapes may be divided into equal parts in many different ways. One simple example uses a rectangle, which can be divided into thirds horizontally, vertically, or with bent lines:

Students can experiment with different ways to equally divide the same shape, using tools such as a geoboard. Recognition that equal shares need not have the same shape lays the groundwork for concepts of area and perimeter that students will focus on in 3rd grade (3.MD.8). This understanding of equal shares will also come into play when students start formal work with fractions, beginning with unit fractions and visual fractional models (3.NF.A). Such connections to more advanced content demonstrate how important it is that students grasp fundamental geometric concepts here in the early elementary grades.

PART III

Lesson Planning and Sample Lesson Plans

CHAPTER 13

Guidance for Instructional Planning

In this chapter, we provide a brief tutorial on designing lesson plans using the types of instructional strategies that appear in this guide's sample lessons. It includes a step-by-step outline for the development of lessons that make best use of proven instructional strategies and will help you ensure students master the new and challenging content represented by the Common Core standards.

The Framework for Instructional Planning

To identify and use effective strategies to develop these lessons, we draw on the instructional planning framework developed for *Classroom Instruction That Works, 2nd edition* (Dean et al., 2012), presented in Figure 13.1.

The Framework organizes nine categories of research-based strategies for increasing student achievement into three components. These components focus on three key aspects of teaching and learning: creating an environment for learning, helping students develop understanding, and helping students extend and apply knowledge. Let's take a closer look at each.

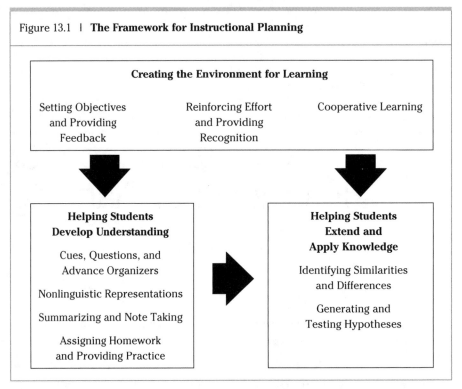

Figure 13.1 | **The Framework for Instructional Planning**

Creating the Environment for Learning

Setting Objectives and Providing Feedback

Reinforcing Effort and Providing Recognition

Cooperative Learning

Helping Students Develop Understanding

Cues, Questions, and Advance Organizers

Nonlinguistic Representations

Summarizing and Note Taking

Assigning Homework and Providing Practice

Helping Students Extend and Apply Knowledge

Identifying Similarities and Differences

Generating and Testing Hypotheses

Source: From *Classroom Instruction That Works, 2nd ed.* (p. xvi) by Ceri Dean, Elizabeth Hubbell, Howard Pitler, and Bj Stone, 2012, Alexandria, VA: ASCD; and Denver, CO: McREL. Copyright 2012 by McREL. Adapted with permission.

Creating the environment for learning

Teachers create a positive environment for learning when they ensure that students are motivated and focused, know what's expected of them, and regularly receive feedback on their progress. When the environment is right, students are actively engaged in their learning and have multiple opportunities to share and discuss ideas with their peers.

A number of instructional strategies that help create a positive environment for learning may be incorporated into the lesson design itself. Other aspects, such as reinforcing effort and providing recognition, may not be a formal part of the lesson plan but are equally important. The following strategies are essential for creating a positive environment for learning:

- Setting objectives and providing feedback
- Reinforcing effort and providing recognition
- Cooperative learning

Helping students develop understanding

This component of the Framework focuses on strategies that are designed to help students work with what they already know and help them integrate new content with their prior understanding. To ensure that students study effectively outside class, teachers also need strategies that support constructive approaches to assigning homework. The strategies that help students develop understanding include the following:

- Cues, questions, and advance organizers
- Nonlinguistic representations
- Summarizing and note taking
- Assigning homework and providing practice

Helping students extend and apply knowledge

In this component of the Framework, teachers use strategies that prompt students to move beyond the "right answers," engage in more complex reasoning, and consider the real-world connections and applications of targeted content and skills, all of which help students gain flexibility when it comes to using what they have learned. The following strategies help students extend and apply knowledge:

- Identifying similarities and differences
- Generating and testing hypotheses

Figure 13.2 illustrates the three major components of teaching and learning described in *Classroom Instruction That Works,* along with the nine types, or categories, of strategies that further define the components and point you toward activities that will suit your learning objectives and support your students' success.

Figure 13.2 | **Framework Components and the Associated Categories of Instructional Strategies**

Component	Category	Definition
Creating the Environment for Learning	Setting Objectives and Providing Feedback	Provide students with a direction for learning and with information about how well they are performing relative to a particular learning objective so they can improve their performance.
	Reinforcing Effort and Providing Recognition	Enhance students' understanding of the relationship between effort and achievement by addressing students' attitudes and beliefs about learning. Provide students with non-material tokens of recognition or praise for their accomplishments related to the attainment of a goal.
	Cooperative Learning	Provide students with opportunities to interact with one another in ways that enhance their learning.
Helping Students Develop Understanding	Cues, Questions, and Advance Organizers	Enhance students' ability to retrieve, use, and organize what they already know about a topic.
	Nonlinguistic Representations • Graphic Organizers • Pictures and Pictographs • Mental Images • Kinesthetic Movement • Models/Manipulatives	Enhance students' ability to represent and elaborate on knowledge using mental images.
	Summarizing and Note Taking	Enhance students' ability to synthesize information and organize it in a way that captures the main ideas and supporting details.
	Providing Practice and Assigning Homework	Extend the learning opportunities for students to practice, review, and apply knowledge. Enhance students' ability to reach the expected level of proficiency for a skill or process.

Figure 13.2	**Framework Components and the Associated Categories of Instructional Strategies (*continued*)**		
Component	Category	Definition
Helping Students Extend and Apply Knowledge	Identifying Similarities and Differences • Comparing • Classifying • Creating/Using Metaphors • Creating/Using Analogies	Enhance students' understanding of and ability to use knowledge by engaging them in mental processes that involve identifying ways in which items are alike and different.
	Generating and Testing Hypotheses	Enhance students' understanding of and ability to use knowledge by engaging them in mental processes that involve making and testing hypotheses.

Source: From *Classroom Instruction That Works, 2nd ed.* (p. xviii) by Ceri Dean, Elizabeth Hubbell, Howard Pitler, and Bj Stone, 2012, Alexandria, VA: ASCD; and Denver, CO: McREL. Copyright 2012 by McREL. Adapted with permission.

Lesson Development, Step by Step

To help you get started developing lessons that incorporate these strategies, we provide a step-by-step process to ensure that you've had an opportunity to consider where within a lesson the various strategies might be used most effectively. Those steps are as follows:

1. Identify the focus for the lesson.
2. Determine how learning will be assessed.
3. Determine the activities that will start the lesson.
4. Determine the activities that will engage students in learning the content.
5. Determine the activities that will close the lesson.

Let's look now at the details of each step and how you might incorporate the nine effective instructional strategies associated with each of the Framework's three components. We'll reference the sample lessons in this guide to illustrate particular aspects of this approach.

Step 1: Identify the focus for the lesson

The critical first step in crafting a lesson is to identify what students should learn as a result of their engagement in the lesson activities. Setting objectives for students also means establishing the guidelines for your development of the lesson—namely, that you will select and develop only those activities that will help students meet the objectives set. A learning objective is built directly from a standard; the objectives found in this guide's sample lessons are constructed from Common Core standards and listed under the heading "Common Core State Standards—Knowledge and Skills to Be Addressed."

Clarifying learning objectives. To ensure that students are clear about what they will learn, you will want your lesson plans to include more specific statements of the objectives in clear, student-friendly language. Some teachers accomplish this by using stems such as "I can…" or "We will be able to…" or "Students will be able to…" and providing a paraphrased version of the standard, simplifying the language as necessary. In the sample lessons for this guide, such specifics may be found under the headings "Knowledge/Vocabulary Objectives" and "Skill/Process Objectives" and prefaced by either "Students will understand…" or "Students will be able to…."

Identifying essential questions and learning objectives. Framing the lesson's objectives under a broader essential question provides students with alternate avenues to find personal relevance and can energize them to seek answers as they begin a unit or lesson. The essential question properly focuses on the broader purpose of learning, and it is most effective when it is open-ended and not a question that can be easily answered. Each of the sample lessons includes an essential question—the learning objectives reframed to clarify for students what value the lesson holds for them.

Identifying foundational knowledge and possible misconceptions related to the learning objectives. As you develop learning objectives for a lesson, consider the other skills students will need to use but that will not be the explicit focus of instruction or assessment. Our discussions of each standard in this guide identify the critical knowledge and skills that students are assumed to have mastered or practiced in lessons prior to learning the new content. In the sample lessons, you'll find these standards under the heading "Common Core State Standards—Prior Knowledge and Skills to Be Applied."

Step 2: Determine how learning will be assessed

As important as identifying the learning objective for a lesson is identifying the criteria you will use to determine if students have met that objective. You will want to be clear about the rigor identified in the Common Core standards. As you develop scoring tools, such as checklists and rubrics that define the various levels of performance related to the objective's knowledge or skill, it is important to review the details of the objective's underlying standard to be sure you are looking for the appropriate level of mastery.

Assessing prior knowledge. Step 2 involves planning how to measure students' prior knowledge, especially the knowledge identified in Step 1 as prerequisite to mastery of the learning objective. For example, you might ask students to complete a short problem or share reflections on their prior experiences with similar tasks. This approach may also surface any lingering student misconceptions that you'll want to address before proceeding.

Providing feedback. This part of the planning process also includes deciding how you will provide students with feedback on their progress toward the outcome. Providing feedback is an important aspect of creating the environment for learning because understanding what good performance looks like, how to judge their own performance relative to a benchmark, and what they need to do to improve their performance helps students develop a sense of control over their learning. During lesson planning, you might also consider how peers can give their classmates feedback on progress toward the stated objective.

Step 3: Determine the activities that will start the lesson

Step 3 of the planning process concerns the sequence of activities at the start of the lesson, which relate to the "Creating the Environment for Learning" component of the Framework for Instructional Planning. The beginning of each lesson should be orchestrated to capture students' interest, communicate the learning objectives, and encourage their commitment to effort.

Communicating learning objectives. You can share learning objectives by stating them orally, but be sure to post them in writing for reference throughout the lesson. Doing so not only reminds the class of the objectives' importance but also ensures that even students who weren't paying close attention or who came in late can identify what they are working to achieve.

Identifying the essential question and providing a context. Students engage in learning more readily when they can see how it connects to their own interests. The essential question you provide at the beginning of the lesson helps orient them to the purpose for learning. Students will also have a greater sense of involvement if you share with them what activities they'll be engaged in and how these activities will help build their understanding and skill. The sample lessons in this guide present this preview under the heading "Activity Description to Share with Students." It is something you might read aloud or post, along with the objectives and essential questions, as you create the environment for learning at the beginning of a lesson. To encourage greater involvement, you might also ask students to set personal goals based on the learning objectives in each activity. These personal goals may translate the learning objective to immediate goals that resonate for each student.

Reinforcing effort. As you develop the activities for the lesson, look for natural points where you might build in opportunities for students to receive the encouragement they need to continue their work. To reinforce student effort, we need to help students understand the direct connection between how hard they work and what they achieve. It's another way in which teachers can provide students with a greater sense of control over their own learning.

Step 4: Determine the activities that will engage students in learning the content

At Step 4 we are at the crux of the lesson, deciding what students will do to acquire, extend, and apply knowledge or skills. This stage of planning includes identifying when formative assessment should take place, when you will provide students feedback from the assessment, and how you will ensure that students have a clear understanding of how they are doing. And, of course, you will need to decide which instructional activities will best serve the lesson's primary purposes, considering whether the activities need to focus on helping students acquire new knowledge and skill or help them extend and refine what they've already learned.

Choosing activities and strategies that develop student understanding. When your aim is to help students understand new information or a new process, then you will want to design activities that incorporate strategies associated with that component of the Framework for Instructional Planning. These are the strategies that help students access prior knowledge and organize new learning. Students come to every lesson with some prior knowledge, and the effective use of strategies such as using cues, questions, and advance organizers can enhance students' ability to retrieve and use what they already know about a topic in order to access something new. You can help students access and leverage their prior knowledge through simple discussion, by providing "KWL"-type advance organizers, by having students read or listen to short texts related to the targeted content, or any other number of ways. Activities incorporating the use of nonlinguistic representations (including visualization) in which students elaborate on knowledge, skills, and processes are other good ways to help students integrate new learning into existing knowledge. The strategies of note taking and summarizing also support students' efforts to synthesize information through the act of organizing it in a way that captures its main ideas and supporting details or highlights key aspects of new processes. Finally, homework can help students learn or review new content and practice skills so that they can more quickly reach the expected level of proficiency. However, you will want to think carefully about your homework practices, as the research on what makes homework effective shows mixed results. Dean and colleagues (2012) recommend that teachers design homework assignments that directly support learning objectives. Students need to understand how homework serves lesson objectives, and once homework is completed, it is important that teachers provide feedback on the assignment.

Choosing activities and strategies that help students extend and apply knowledge. When your aim is to help students extend or apply their knowledge or master skills and processes, they will need opportunities to practice independently. What are beneficial are activities that involve making comparisons, classifying, and creating or using metaphors and analogies. Research summarized in the second edition of *Classroom Instruction That Works* indicates that these strategies, associated with the "Helping Students Extend and Apply Knowledge" component of the Framework for Instructional Planning, are a worthwhile use of instructional time. They help raise students' levels of understanding and improve their ability to use what they learn. Because students need to understand the concepts or skills that they're comparing, you are more likely to insert these activities later in a lesson than at the outset.

Remember, too, that strategies that help students generate and test hypotheses are not meant just for science classrooms. They are a way to deepen students' knowledge by requiring them to use critical-thinking skills, such as analysis and evaluation.

Grouping students for activities. Cooperative learning can be tremendously beneficial, whether students are developing a new skill or understanding or applying or extending it. With every lesson you design, consider when it makes sense to use this strategy, what kind of student grouping will be most beneficial, and how these groups should be composed. Cooperative learning is a strong option, for example, when you want to differentiate an activity based on student readiness, interest, or learning style. Consider, too, that students' learning experiences will be different depending on whether you permit them to self-select into groups of their choosing or assign their group partners, whether the groups are larger (four or five students) or smaller (e.g., pair work), and whether these groups are homogeneous or heterogeneous.

Providing students with the opportunity to share and discuss their ideas with one another in varying cooperative learning arrangements lays a foundation for the world beyond school, which depends on people working interdependently to solve problems and to innovate. Interacting with one another also deepens students' knowledge of the concepts they are learning; in other words, talking about ideas and listening to others' ideas helps students understand a topic and retain what they've learned, and it may send their thinking in interesting new directions.

Step 5: Determine the activities that will close the lesson

Bringing the lesson to a close provides an opportunity for you and students to look back on and sum up the learning experience.

During this part of the lesson, you want to return to the learning objectives and confirm that you have addressed each of them. This can be approached in one or more ways—through informal sharing, formative assessment, or even summative assessment. Students benefit from the opportunity to gauge their progress in learning. You might prompt them to reflect on the lesson in a journal entry, learning log, or response card, which can easily serve as an informal check for understanding. Note that asking students to share what they found most difficult as well as what worked well can provide you with insight you can apply during the next lesson and can use to refine the lesson just completed.

Depending upon the nature of the objective and whether the lesson appears late in the unit, you may elect to conduct a formal summative assessment. Alternatively, you may identify a homework assignment tied to the learning objective, making sure that students understand how the assignment will help them deepen their understanding or develop their skill.

* * *

In the remaining pages of this guide, we offer sample lesson plans based on the Common Core standards for both English language arts/literacy and mathematics, the Framework for Instructional Planning, and the steps just outlined.

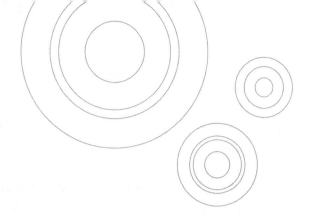

Understanding Author and Illustrator Purpose in Books About Plants and Seeds

Course: Kindergarten ELA/Science
Length of Lesson: Two hours; six 20-minute class periods

Introduction

Many young children first learn about print by sitting and listening to books read to them by parents, guardians, and older siblings. They are exposed to text by attending story time at the local library, watching television shows such as PBS's *Super Why,* and using interactive computer games such as Word World. Emergent literacy—or what students glean about reading and writing behaviors from these early experiences with text—lays the foundation for the lessons taught in classrooms.

If students are going to be prepared for the demands set forth in the Common Core standards, then young readers will need many opportunities to interact with a variety of texts, and they must have conversations about those texts that deepen their knowledge about print concepts and the purposes for reading.

In this lesson, which is spread out over several class periods, kindergarten students will focus on learning the roles of book authors and illustrators and combine this knowledge with the understanding that we read to obtain information. This awareness will contribute to the foundation that students need to become independent and thoughtful readers. This lesson also includes an explicit focus on science content, specifically information about seeds and plants. This cross-curricular emphasis at the kindergarten level is something of a departure from the norm.

Strategies from the Framework for Instructional Planning

- *Creating the Environment for Learning:* Each class period starts with an opportunity for students to reflect on and discuss the lesson's essential questions (see p. 170). This aspect of instruction helps students to understand what they will be learning and how they will go about it. The several essential questions in this lesson are designed to trigger students' curiosity about why authors write books and why illustrators create the pictures that accompany an author's text.
- *Helping Students Develop Understanding:* In this lesson, practice time is the primary strategy used to help students develop understanding. They will have multiple opportunities to practice identifying authors and illustrators. They will also collaborate with a partner and share what they have learned about the topics that are discussed in the stories they hear.
- *Helping Students Extend and Apply Knowledge:* Students will extend and apply knowledge by comparing the authors' purposes and illustrators' purposes across books about a similar topic.

Common Core State Standards—Knowledge and Skills to Be Addressed

Strand/Domain: Reading Informational Text

Heading: Key Ideas and Details

RI.K.2 With prompting and support, ask and answer questions about key details in a text.

Heading: Craft and Structure

RI.K.6 Name the author and illustrator of a text and define the role of each in presenting the ideas or information in a text.

Heading: Integration of Knowledge and Ideas

RI.K.7 With prompting and support, describe the relationship between illustrations and the text in which they appear (e.g., what person, place, thing, or idea in the text an illustration depicts).

Strand/Domain: Reading Foundational Skills

Heading: Print Concepts

RF.K.1 Demonstrate understanding of the organization and basic features of print.

a. Follow words from left to right, top to bottom, and page by page.

b. Understand that words are separated by spaces in print.

c. Recognize and name all upper- and lowercase letters of the alphabet.

Heading: Phonics and Word Recognition

RF.K.3 Know and apply grade-level phonics and word analysis skills in decoding words.

c. Read common high-frequency words by sight (e.g., *the, of, to, you, she, my, is, are, do, does*).

Strand: Writing

Heading: Text Types and Purposes

W.K.2 Use a combination of drawing, dictating, and writing to compose informative/explanatory texts in which they name what they are writing about and supply some information about the topic.

Common Core State Standards—Prior Knowledge and Skills to Be Applied

Strand/Domain: Reading Informational Text

Heading: Craft and Structure

RI.K.5 Identify the front cover, back cover, and title page of a book.

Strand: Speaking and Listening

Heading: Comprehension and Collaboration

SL.K.1 Participate in collaborative conversations with diverse partners about kindergarten topics and texts with peers and adults in small and larger groups.

a. Follow agreed-upon rules for discussions (e.g., listening to others and taking turns speaking about the topics and texts under discussion).

b. Continue a conversation through multiple exchanges.

Strand/Domain: Reading Foundational Skills

Heading: Print Concepts

RF.K.1 Demonstrate understanding of the organization and basic features of print.

b. Recognize that spoken words are represented in written language by specific sequences of letters.

Teacher's Lesson Summary

In this lesson, students will have an opportunity to listen to and discuss two different texts about seeds and plants over the course of several class periods. Each book has a different author and a different illustrator. By listening to and discussing the set of texts, students will develop an understanding of why authors write books and why illustrators create pictures to accompany the text in books. Fostering an understanding of author and illustrator purpose will support students as they develop the skill of using text and pictures to build knowledge.

Essential Questions: What do book authors and illustrators do? How do authors and illustrators help us learn new information? How do drawing, writing, and telling someone what I have learned help me as a reader? How does knowing about which way to read, knowing about spaces and upper- and lowercase letters, help me know what to do when I read a book? Why is it important to know high-frequency words?

Learning Objective: To learn how authors and illustrators provide information in text and pictures.

Knowledge/Vocabulary Objectives

At the conclusion of this lesson, students will understand

• The purposes of an author and an illustrator.

• The meanings of the high-frequency words that appear in the targeted texts.

Skill/Process Objectives

At the conclusion of this lesson, students will be able to

• Use the text and pictures to support learning.

• Ask and answer questions about key details in each story.

• Draw, dictate, or write to explain knowledge about a topic.

• Make a connection between information learned and the texts read.

Resources/Preparation Needed

• Required texts: *Green and Growing: A Book About Plants* written by Susan Black-aby and illustrated by Charlene DeLage; *What Kinds of Seeds Are These?* written by Heidi Bee Roemer and illustrated by Olena Kassian
• Chart paper or an interactive whiteboard
• Sharing-partner assignments that support behavioral expectations; consider matching students based on developmental reading levels such that like-ability students are paired together
• A prepared response sheet (see **Figure A: Student Response Sheet,** p. 177) to help students capture and reflect on their learning that includes space for pictures and writing and the titles of the two required texts supporting this lesson, one per student

Activity Description to Share with Students

Authors write books to share information about different things or to tell a story. Many books also have pictures that help explain what the author is writing about. Good readers will use the pictures to help them understand the author's message.

Over the new few days, you will hear two stories about seeds and plants. Each story was written by one author and illustrated by a person who makes pictures, who is called an *illustrator*. You will think about why each author wrote the story and why each illustrator drew the pictures. Knowing what authors and illustrators do and why they do it can help you when you want to learn new and different information.

Lesson Activity Sequence—Class #1: Reading to Discern the Author's Purpose

Start the Lesson

1. Ask students to share what they think an author does.
2. Ask students to share the names of their favorite books.
3. Write the titles on chart paper or a whiteboard.

4. Ask students to tell you the names of the authors who wrote these favorite books, if they can remember. Write the author names next to the book titles.

5. Ask students why they think the authors wrote these books. What was each author's *purpose*?

6. Explain that today you are going to read a story about plants. Ask the students to listen to the story and think about why the author may have written the text.

Engage Students in Learning the Content

1. Read aloud *Green and Growing: A Book About Plants* written by Susan Blackaby and illustrated by Charlene DeLage.

2. After the reading, ask students why they think the author wrote the book, and tell them to share their responses with their sharing partner.

3. Ask several pairs of students to share their conclusions about why the author wrote the book, and record their responses in the "Author's Purpose" column of a table set up as follows:

Title/Author Name/ Illustrator Name	Author's Purpose	Illustrator's Purpose

4. Validate the students' responses.

Close the Lesson

Tell students that you will reread *Green and Growing* again tomorrow, and when they listen to the story next time, they will be paying close attention to the pictures.

Lesson Activity Sequence—Class #2: Reading to Discern the Illustrator's Purpose

Additional Resources/Preparation Needed

In advance of the lesson, collect several of the favorite books that students shared during Class #1, choosing texts to represent a variety of authors and illustrators.

Start the Lesson

1. Ask students to share what they know about book illustrators.
2. Show students the books that you collected—a representative sample of the favorites they named the day before. Connect these books to titles on the chart paper/whiteboard list of favorites from Class #1. Add the author's name next to the associated titles (if you did not have the author listed previously), and revise any incorrect author names.
3. Draw the students' attention to the illustrators' names. Explain to students what an illustrator does, making connections between what the students shared about illustrators a few minutes before.
4. Write the names of the favorite books' illustrators next to the book titles.
5. Ask students why they think illustrators make pictures for books.
6. Explain that today you are going to reread the story you read in Class #1. Ask the students to listen to the story, paying close attention to the illustrations.

Engage Students in Learning the Content

1. Reread aloud *Green and Growing: A Book About Plants* by Susan Blackaby and Charlene DeLage.
2. While reading, point to examples that show the connection between the text and the pictures. For example, the text on page 6 reads, "A plant can be a tree or a shrub. A plant can be a flower or a trailing vine." The illustration that spans pages 6 and 7 shows a tree, many flowers, plants, and a flowering plant growing up a trellis. Similarly, the text on page 16 reads, "Plants can grow almost any-where." Pictures on pages 16 and 17 reflect plants growing in the desert, near mountains, in water, and in the forest.

3. After reading, ask students why they think the illustrator drew the particular pictures she did to go with the words in the text. Tell students to share their responses with their sharing partner.

4. Ask several pairs to share their conclusions about why the illustrator drew these pictures, and record their responses in the "Illustrator's Purpose" column of the Author and Illustrator Purpose table you created the previous day.

5. Validate the students' responses.

Close the Lesson

1. Tell students that during the next lesson you will read *Green and Growing* one more time. Their job will be to listen specifically for information about plants.

2. Remind students that rereading is a strategy that good readers use to learn.

Lesson Activity Sequence—Class #3: Reading for Information

Start the Lesson

1. Review the purpose of a book author and illustrator.

2. Review the Author and Illustrator Purpose table, retelling what the students shared in the previous two classes about the author's purpose and the illustrator's purpose communicated in *Green and Growing: A Book About Plants.*

3. Remind students that one reason we read is to obtain information, and authors and illustrators develop their work in a way that helps us learn. When possible, make connections to the student responses recorded in the table.

4. Tell students that they will do a shared reading of *Green and Growing* and that you will ask them to explain what they've learned about plants using what they remember from their multiple readings of the story and the pictures that support the text.

Engage Students in Learning the Content

1. Reread *Green and Growing* aloud with assistance from the students. Focus on the particular print concepts (e.g., directionality, words separated by spaces, upper- and lowercase letters) and high-frequency (e.g., *the, to, is*) words that reflect the needs of the students.

2. When the reading is complete, ask students to turn to their partner and share one or two facts they remember from the story. They should also identify which pictures helped them remember this information.
3. Ask several pairs to share what they learned from the text. As they do so, flip to sections in the book they are referring to and prompt them to make connections between what they remember and the illustrations that support the text.
4. Validate the students' responses.

Close the Lesson

Remind students that we read to increase our understanding of information. Tell them that during the next lesson, you will read another book about plants and seeds so that they can see how different authors and illustrators write books about the same topic.

Lesson Activity Sequence—Class #4: Reading to Discern the Author's Purpose

Repeat the activities of Class #1 with the new text, *What Kinds of Seeds Are These?* written by Heidi Bee Roemer and illustrated by Olena Kassian.

Lesson Activity Sequence—Class #5: Reading to Discern the Illustrator's Purpose

Repeat the activities of Class #2 with the new text.

Lesson Activity Sequence—Class #6: Reading for Information

Start the Lesson

1. Review the purpose of a book author and illustrator.
2. Review the Author and Illustrator Purpose table for *What Kinds of Seeds Are These?*
3. Remind students that we read to obtain information, and authors and illustrators develop this information in a way that helps us learn.
4. Tell students that they will do a shared reading of *What Kinds of Seeds Are These?* After the reading, you will ask them to share what they've learned about seeds from the text and from the pictures that support the text.

Engage Students in Learning the Content

1. Reread *What Kinds of Seeds Are These?* aloud with assistance from the students, again focusing on print concepts and high-frequency words that meet students' needs.

2. Ask students to share one or two facts they remember from the story and think about which pictures helped them remember what they learned. Tell students to share their responses with their sharing partner, keeping in mind that their responses must reflect key details from the text. In other words, what the students share should connect closely to the text they've read.

3. Remind students about the previous book, *Green and Growing.*

4. Introduce and distribute the **Student Response Sheet** (see Figure A, p. 177), giving one to each student. Tell students that they will work with their partner to think about what they learned about seeds and plants from the two books, *Green and Growing* and *What Kinds of Seeds Are These?* Then they will work on their own to capture what they learned in writing. Remind students that they can write using letters, words, and pictures. Consider modeling this activity to give students additional support. Ask students to circle the title of the book that helped them learn the most about plants and seeds.

Close the Lesson

Give students time to share their writing. Collect students' work, and consider the assessment data their oral and written responses provide. For example, students may need additional assistance identifying key ideas from the text they read rather than sharing knowledge learned from alternative sources.

Additional Resources for This Lesson

More information about author and illustrator purpose can be found in *Creating Literacy Instruction for All Students* by Thomas G. Gunning and at the website Readwritethink.org.

Figure A | **Student Response Sheet**

My Name _____

What I learned about plants and seeds:

The book that taught me *the most* about plants and seeds was

Green and Growing   *What Kinds of Seeds Are These?*

Reader's Theater and Lon Po Po

Course: 1st grade ELA
Length of Lesson: Two hours; three 40-minute class periods

Introduction

The "Note on Range and Content of Student Reading" within the introduction to the Common Core standards for ELA states, "Through extensive reading of stories, dramas, poems, and myths from diverse cultures and different time periods, students gain literacy and cultural knowledge as well as familiarity with various text structures and elements" (CCSSI, 2010c, p. 10).

This three-part lesson for 1st grade highlights diverse reading material and includes the kind of multiple experiences with text that children must have in order to become proficient readers. Students will reread and think about a Chinese version of the familiar children's story "Little Red Riding Hood." Through their interactions with the text, they will practice identifying story elements and build their capacity to understand basic story elements. Students will then use their growing knowledge of story elements to write a short play and then perform their play to practice their reading fluency.

Strategies from the Framework for Instructional Planning

- *Creating the Environment for Learning:* Each of the class periods for this lesson begins with an opportunity to highlight the essential questions for students. The essential questions are written in kid-friendly language to ensure the learning objective is accessible. Students also will work collaboratively to write and then perform a short play, which will create an engaging context for learning.

- *Helping Students Develop Understanding:* Students will use their prior knowledge of story elements to help them understand a story that is read aloud to them. They will use a graphic organizer to express what they know about the story.

- *Helping Students Extend and Apply Knowledge:* Students will extend and apply their understanding by writing a script that is similar to but not an exact replication of the read-aloud story. By adapting the story elements map to write the script, students will engage in analysis, a critical-thinking skill.

Common Core State Standards—Knowledge and Skills to Be Addressed

Strand/Domain: Reading Literature
Heading: Key Ideas and Details
RL.1.2 Retell stories, including key details, and demonstrate understanding of their central message or lesson.

Strand/Domain: Reading Foundational Skills
Heading: Fluency
RF.1.4 Read with sufficient accuracy and fluency to support comprehension.
b. Read on-level text orally with accuracy, appropriate rate, and expression on successive readings.

Strand: Writing
Heading: Text Types and Purposes
W.1.3 Write narratives in which they recount two or more appropriately sequenced events, include some details regarding what happened, use temporal words to signal event order, and provide some sense of closure.

Common Core State Standards—Prior Knowledge and Skills to Be Applied

Strand: Speaking and Listening
Heading: Comprehension and Collaboration
SL.1.1 Participate in collaborative conversations with diverse partners about grade 1 topics and texts with peers and adults in small and larger groups.

a. Follow agreed-upon rules for discussions (e.g., listening to others with care, speaking one at a time about the topics and texts under discussion).

b. Build on others' talk in conversations by responding to the comments of others through multiple exchanges.

Teacher's Lesson Summary

In this lesson, 1st grade students will focus on *Lon Po Po: A Red-Riding Hood Story from China*. Although many of the students will be familiar with the general plot of the story, they will need to listen carefully to pick up and capture the nuanced differences between *Lon Po Po* and the Little Red Riding Hood story that they know. Through multiple readings, students will practice retelling the important details to reach a satisfying conclusion and demonstrate their comprehension of the story. Then they will translate their understanding of the basic story elements into a script that they will prepare to perform for their peers.

Reader's theater is sometimes criticized for the limited amount of fluency practice afforded all students in the production (Shanahan, 2005). This lesson addresses that drawback by challenging students to make sure every cast member has the same number of lines. Finally, students will practice their lines and put on performances.

Essential Questions: Why is it important to understand story elements? How does writing a short play based on a story help me understand the story better? How does practicing a play help me become a better reader?

Learning Objective: To learn how to read and understand a story.

Knowledge/Vocabulary Objective

At the conclusion of this lesson, students will understand

• Story elements—specifically, characters, setting, major events, and an ending that provides a sense of closure.

Skill/Process Objectives

At the conclusion of this lesson, students will be able to

• Retell a story with sufficient details.

- Use feedback to write and read aloud a script that captures major events in a story.
- Use reader's theater to support reading aloud accurately, correctly, and with expression.

Resources/Preparation Needed

- Required text: *Lon Po Po: A Red-Riding Hood Story from China*, translated and illustrated by Ed Young; students should have heard this story read aloud at least once prior to the lesson's start
- A prepared story elements map (see p. 182), which will serve as an advance organizer
- Prepared small-group assignments for the reader's theater script writing (we recommend groups of four, composed to include a range of reading abilities and to ensure that behavioral expectations can be met)
- A collection of short scripts that students can use as models for the script-writing activity; these are available in many reading textbooks, and the PBS Kids website (http://pbskids.org/zoom/activities/playhouse/) contains sample scripts

Activity Description to Share with Students

Many stories are organized in ways that present clues to help you understand what is happening and even help you predict what will happen next. These clues are called *story elements*.

One story element is *characters*. Most stories have characters. Characters can be people, animals, and even things. The characters do things in the story. In "The Three Little Pigs," for example, the pigs build houses made from different materials. Stories also have *settings*. A setting is where the story takes place. When the characters do things in the story, these are called *events*. Finally, stories have an *ending*, and that ending should be satisfying to the person who reads or hears the story.

In this lesson, you will use story elements—characters, a setting, major events, and an ending—to write a script for reader's theater. The play you will write will be based on the story we have read, *Lon Po Po: A Red-Riding Hood Story from China*. You will work in a small group to retell the story of Lon Po Po and work with the others in your group to make sure you have included all the story elements. After you write your script, you and the classmates in your group will practice presenting the play, just as if you were on stage in a theater. After you've practiced, you will present your play to the whole class. Practicing your parts will help you read smoothly and with feeling.

Lesson Activity Sequence—Class #1: Mapping Story Elements

Start the Lesson

1. Post the essential questions and discuss the learning objective.
2. Tell students that you will reread the story *Lon Po Po: A Red-Riding Hood Story from China.*
3. Ask students to tell you what they remember about the story based on your previous reading.
4. Using chart paper, an overhead, or an interactive whiteboard, post a copy of a prepared story element map, like one shown here:

Characters	Setting
Major Events	**Ending**

Tell students that today they will listen to the story of Lon Po Po with the goal of identifying the four story elements shown—characters, the setting, major events, and an ending—and being able to fill in the map.

Engage Students in Learning the Content

1. Read aloud *Lon Po Po: A Red-Riding Hood Story from China.*
2. Ask students to turn to a sharing partner and identify the story elements needed to complete the story element map.
3. Ask students to retell the characters and setting. Listen for the most salient characters (the wolf, Shang, Tao, and Paotze) and settings (the house and the tree). Explain to students that while the character of the mother and setting of the country are important, the majority of the story takes place in the house and the tree, and the major characters are the three sisters and the wolf.
4. Ask students to tell you the major events in the story, in the order they happened. Make a list of their responses on chart paper.

   Possible events students might offer:
   - Mother went to visit the grandmother.
   - A wolf knocked on the door.
   - One sister asked why the wolf's voice sounded funny.
   - The wolf got a basket.
   - The sisters tricked the wolf and climbed a tree.
   - The wolf died.
   - Mother came home.

5. Help students distinguish between *minor events* (e.g., one of the sisters listened through the door) and *major events* (e.g., the sisters tricked the wolf and climbed a tree). Circle, highlight, or otherwise distinguish the major events, and transfer them to the story elements map.
6. Ask students to tell you how the story ended. Help them evaluate the ending to make sure that it brings a sense of closure. For example, the students might say, "The wolf died." Although the wolf dies, this ending does not describe what happened to the three sisters. Make sure that students understand that a reader or listener would probably want to know what happened to the sisters; having that information is what makes for a satisfying ending.

Close the Lesson

1. Model retelling the story based on the story elements map.

2. Ask students to practice retelling the story with their sharing partner, using the story elements map as a reference.

3. Tell students that tomorrow, they will be working in small groups to start writing their scripts for reader's theater.

Lesson Activity Sequence—Class #2: Writing a Script

Start the Lesson

1. Review the essential questions, and tell students that today they will focus on the second question: *How does writing a short play based on a story help me understand the story better?*

2. Review the story elements map, highlighting the characters, settings, major events, and ending.

3. Give students their small-group assignments. Explain that they will work in these small groups to write their scripts.

4. Remind students about scripts for plays that they have seen before, and distribute copies of model scripts, if you are using them.

Engage Students in Learning the Content

1. Tell students that when they write their scripts it's important for every person in the group to have at least one part and that all students must have the same number of lines to say. If this task proves difficult, consider asking students to write the script with the understanding that several of them may choral-read different parts. In other words, several voices will combine to equal one character.

2. Tell students that although the story has three sisters, it is OK for them to change the sisters into *sisters and brothers* or *brothers*, based on who is in the group. Remind students that they want to retell the major events in the story and presenting those major events is more important than having all the characters be girls.

3. Remind students that the lines they write are words that the character would say. For example, the wolf might say something like, "Please let me in. I'm your Po Po," rather than, "The wolf asked the girls to let him in."

4. Students will use the class period to write a draft of the script, using the story elements map to guide them.

5. Provide guidance as needed.

Close the Lesson

1. Gather the students and ask several to share a line from their script. Ask the rest of the class to listen to make sure that the line is something that the character would say.
2. Tell students that they will use the next class period to practice with their scripts.

Lesson Activity Sequence—Class #3: Play Practice

Start the Lesson

1. Gather students and remind them of the lesson's essential questions. This time, focus their attention on the third question: *How does practicing a play help me become a better reader?*
2. Tell students that they will practice their plays during class. They should not try to memorize their parts; rather, they should practice reading their lines with one another so that their reading sounds like talking. This practice will help their fluency.
3. Model a couple of line readings that do not sound like people talking and that lack feeling or emotional expression. Then provide a couple of examples that demonstrate prosody.

Engage Students in Learning the Content

1. Give students time to practice performing their scripts.
2. Observe the groups and provide guidance as needed.
3. Remind students in the group to listen to one another to make sure that their reading sounds like talking.

Close the Lesson/Reflect on Learning

1. Gather students and ask them to share their responses to the following questions with their sharing partner:

   • *Why is it important to identify the characters, setting, major events, and ending in stories?*

• *How does this information help me as a reader?*

2. Solicit responses from the students, and consider the assessment data these responses provide. For example, students might indicate that characters help them keep track of who is in a story and what happens to them.

3. Tell students that they will perform their plays during the next class period.

Additional Resources for This Lesson

Additional information about reader's theater can be found in R. G. Chatel's article "Developing Reading Fluency: An Abundance of Technology Resources" in the January 2005 issue of the *New England Reading Association Journal* and at www.reading. org.

Reading Soap Bubbles and Practicing the Habits of Effective Readers

Course: 2nd grade ELA
Length of Lesson: Two hours; three 40-minute class periods

Introduction

The Common Core standards make it clear that students require multiple opportunities to engage with increasingly complex texts during their K–12 school experience. Students must also be able to use writing to explain what they have learned. The standards also note that elementary school students, particularly those in the primary grades, need more classroom time devoted to reading and discussing informational text. The current paucity of such experiences for young students limits their opportunities to develop the skills they need to comprehend the information they find in textbooks, opinion pieces, technical reports, and other kinds of nonfiction texts. The Common Core promotes literacy across the curriculum, encouraging students at all levels to engage with complex informational texts that support higher learning in the content areas, including science.

In this lesson, students will read a selection about water and soap bubbles from a nonfiction book that is cited in Appendix B to the Common Core ELA standards as an exemplar text for grades 2–3. Through experimentation, shared reading, and responding to questions about some basic scientific principles they have learned, students will practice the habits of effective readers. They also will practice skimming, which is a useful advance organizer that promotes comprehension.

Strategies from the Framework for Instructional Planning

- *Creating the Environment for Learning:* It is essential to set objectives for student learning when creating the environment for learning. This lesson begins with a review of the essential questions to prepare students for the learning opportunities ahead. In addition, students will have to put forth effort to understand and explain the complicated concept of surface tension and its relationship to soap bubbles. Reinforcing students' efforts to explain this concept will support their willingness to take on more difficult tasks.
- *Helping Students Develop Understanding:* Students will be asked to access their prior knowledge about soap bubbles. They then will integrate the new knowledge they obtain from reading and conducting experiments and be asked to explain the connections.
- *Helping Students Extend and Apply Knowledge:* Students will extend, apply, and demonstrate the knowledge and understanding they acquire in this lesson by asking and answering questions about soap bubbles.

Common Core State Standards—Knowledge and Skills to Be Addressed

Strand/Domain: Reading Informational Text
Heading: Craft and Structure

RI.2.5 Know and use various text features (e.g., captions, bold print, subheadings, glossaries, indexes, electronic menus, icons) to locate key facts or information in a text efficiently.

RI.2.6 Identify the main purpose of a text, including what the author wants to answer, explain, or describe.

Heading: Integration of Knowledge and Ideas

RI.2.7 Explain how specific images (e.g., diagram showing how a machine works) contribute to and clarify a text.

Strand: Writing
Heading: Research to Build and Present Knowledge

W.2.8 Recall information from experiences or gather information from provided sources to answer a question.

Common Core State Standards—Prior Knowledge and Skills to Be Applied

Strand/Domain: Reading Informational Text

Heading: Key Ideas and Details

RI.2.1 Ask and answer such questions as who, what, where, when, why, and how to demonstrate understanding of key details in a text.

Teacher's Lesson Summary

Over the course of three class sessions, students will practice several skills that effective readers use. They will learn about skimming a text before reading it, which entails focusing on text features such as headings and pictures. Students will also practice using writing to share what they have learned, and this will include identifying the source of their knowledge. The students' reading and writing experiences will be supported by hands-on experimentation with soap bubbles, which will bring in some basic scientific concepts and principles.

Essential Questions: How do images help me understand the text? What clues from the text can I use to help me describe what the author is trying to explain? How does responding to questions in writing help me remember what I've read and what I've seen?

Learning Objective: To learn from informational texts by skimming, reading carefully, asking questions through experiments, and writing and talking about what we have learned.

Knowledge/Vocabulary Objectives

At the conclusion of these lessons, students will understand

- The concept of a sphere.
- The concept of surface tension.
- How pictures and other text features highlight information in books.

Skill/Process Objectives

At the conclusion of this lesson, students will be able to

- Skim text and use images to support learning.
- Ask and answer questions based on what they have read and what they have experienced.

Resources/Preparation Needed

- Required text: *A Drop of Water* by Walter Wick
- An enlarged copy of pages 14–15 ("Soap Bubbles") in *A Drop of Water,* which will support a shared reading experience
- Copies of the "Soap Bubbles" section, one per student
- Various materials for soap bubble experimentation, including a prepared soap solution (made according to the directions on pages 38–39 of *A Drop of Water*), pie pans to hold the solution, pipe cleaners molded into circles to serve as bubble blowers, clear plastic cups, plastic straws, and paper towels
- A prepared KWL chart (see p. 191)
- Prepared small-group assignments (3–4 students, grouped to support behavioral expectations) for the soap bubble experimentation (see p. 191)
- Student science journals
- A set of kid-friendly definitions for the following terms: *sphere, surface,* and *surface tension*

Activity Description to Share with Students

Good readers use many strategies to help them read. The way a book is organized can give you clues about what to expect. The pictures also can make it easier for you to understand what the author is trying to explain. Authors who write books about information use a variety of tools such as headings, captions, drawings, photographs, and diagrams to convey their message. In addition to understanding this kind of text structure, good readers often write about what they've learned. Writing can help you remember the topic that you read about and clarify what you understand and don't understand about the topic.

This lesson is based on a selection about soap bubbles from the book *A Drop of Water.* You will learn how to skim the book, which means "use the pictures and captions to help you predict the information you will find when you read." You also will have the opportunity to experiment with soap bubbles and record what you learn. Finally, you will use what you have learned from the reading passage and your observations about bubbles from your experiments to answer questions in your science journal.

Lesson Activity Sequence—Class #1: Playing with Bubbles

Start the Lesson

1. Post the essential questions and discuss the learning objectives.
2. Ask students to tell you what they know about soap bubbles. You may prompt them by telling them to think about the bubbles that they see while taking a bath or when washing the dishes. Record their responses in the first column of a posted KWL chart, like the one pictured:

What We **K**now	What We **W**ant to Know	What We Learned

3. Ask students to tell you what they want to know or learn about bubbles. Record their responses in the second column of the KWL chart.
4. Tell students that you will give them an opportunity to experiment with bubbles. At the end of the class period, everyone will come back together, and they will share what they've learned.
5. Solicit responses about what the students need to do to be safe with the materials.

Engage Students in Learning the Content

1. Show students how to use pipe cleaners and plastic cups to create bubbles with the soap bubble solution that you poured into the pie pans.
2. Give the students ample opportunity, at least 15 minutes, to experiment with the bubbles and then clean up. You may want to give the students some suggestions

about various things they can do with the materials, but they should use the time to try a variety of different things.

Close the Lesson

1. Bring the students back together, and ask volunteers to share what they learned as they experimented with bubbles. Record their responses in the third column of the KWL chart.
2. Tell students that during the next class session, they will be reading about soap bubbles.

Lesson Activity Sequence—Class #2: Skimming and Reading

Start the Lesson

1. Review the first two essential questions: *How do images help me understand the text? What clues from the text can I use to help me describe what the author is trying to explain?*
2. Tell students that you are going to teach them a strategy that good readers use to help them anticipate what they are going to read about. The strategy is called *skimming.*
3. Tell students that skimming is a way of looking at the text without focusing on all of the words. They can look at the pictures and the headings, which often are darker so that they stand out.
4. Page through a copy of *A Drop of Water*, pointing out the pictures and reading the headings.
5. Ask students to tell you what types of information they think they would learn from reading the entire book. Validate their responses by asking them which pictures or headings support their replies.

Engage Students in Learning the Content

1. Display the large copy of "Soap Bubbles."
2. Ask students to tell you about the pictures and the heading they see. Ask them to predict what they will learn about soap bubbles as they read the text.
3. Tell students that you are going to read the text to them and then you are going to read it a second time together.

4. Read the text, pointing to the line as you read.

5. Highlight the following words and phrases related to the scientific content: *sphere, surface,* and *surface tension.*

6. Ask students to draw connections between what they heard and what they remember from their experiments with bubbles. Pay particular attention to the students' use of the content-related words and phrases.

7. Read the text aloud again, pointing to each line. Ask the students to read along with you.

Close the Lesson

1. Give students their individual copies of the "Soap Bubbles" reading.

2. Ask students to practice explaining the selection to a partner. For example, students can review the heading, look at the pictures, and run their fingers over the text selection looking for words they find interesting. Students also may retell what they remember from the reading and practice locating related text in the selection.

Lesson Activity Sequence—Class #3: Sharing Learning Through Writing

Start the Lesson

1. Gather the students and remind them of the final essential question: *How does responding to questions in writing help me remember what I've read and what I've seen?*

2. Remind students that good readers often use writing to help them understand and remember what they've read.

3. Tell students that they will use what they've read and what they remember from their experiments with soap bubbles to answer questions about what they've learned.

Engage Students in Learning the Content

1. Tell students that they will write their responses to the questions in their science journals. Display the following questions:

   A. *What do you know about spheres? Aside from the bubbles, where else do you see spheres?*

B. *Plain water bubbles break easily, but soap bubbles can stretch without breaking. Why do soap bubbles stretch?*

C. *What do you now know about soap bubbles that you did not know before?*

2. Tell students to make sure they write down the source for every answer that they give. For example, if they learned about spheres from the book, they should write "book" next to their answer to Question A. If they learned why soap bubbles stretch from the experiment, they should write "experiment" next to their answer to Question B.

3. Give students time to answer the questions in their journals. Remind them to use the conventions of standard English in their responses.

4. Provide guidance as needed.

Close the Lesson

1. Bring students together and ask them to share their written responses, including the source of their learning, with their sharing partners.

2. Solicit several responses from the students and consider the assessment data the responses provide. For example, students may have difficulty determining the source for their answers, or you may need to help them understand that there might be two sources for their answers (e.g., book and experiment).

Additional Resources for This Lesson

Additional information about soap bubbles (for teachers and students) can be found at http://dsc.discovery.com/tv-shows/other-shows/videos/time-warp-soap-in-microwave.htm and www.exploratorium.edu/ronh/bubbles/soap.html

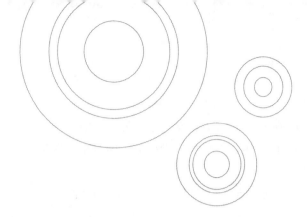

Decomposing Numbers up to 10 into Pairs

Course: Kindergarten Mathematics
Length of Lesson: Five or more 45-minute class periods

Introduction

To understand algebra, students must develop a strong number sense. The Common Core standards for mathematics begin this preparation in students' first year of schooling, stating that more learning time in kindergarten should be devoted to number sense than to other topics (CCSSI, 2010g).

Foundations for Success: The Final Report of the National Mathematics Advisory Panel (2008) identifies three clusters of concepts and skills as critical foundations to mastering algebra. One of these foundations, fluency with whole numbers, including the "ability to compose and decompose whole numbers" (p. 45), is a useful summary of the standard that is central to this lesson (K.OA.A.3).

In addition to helping students understand and solidify mastery of decomposing numbers up to and including 10, the lesson's extended time frame and practice-focused structure—which has students working with teacher guidance, in cooperative groups, and independently on various short-duration tasks in mathematics learning centers—also provide students with many opportunities to improve their number fluency and problem-solving skills. Such a focus is a central concern of the National Mathematics Advisory Panel's *Foundations for Success*, which notes that "conceptual understanding of mathematical operations, fluent execution of procedures, and fast access to number combinations together support effective and efficient problem solving" (2008, p. 26).

Strategies from the Framework for Instructional Planning

- *Creating the Environment for Learning:* This lesson includes an essential question and learning objective (see p. 198) to be posted in the classroom and emphasized continually with students. It features a variety of grouping contexts—whole group, cooperative groups, and independent learning—as well as many instructional approaches, including direct and guided instruction, differentiation, mathematical discourse, problem solving, cooperative learning, independent practice, and ongoing formative assessment. Students receive feedback from the teacher, from peers, and (optionally) from interactive technology. The learning center structure allows the teacher opportunities for individual conferencing to assess student understanding and provide individual corrective feedback.
- *Helping Students Develop Understanding:* Nonlinguistic representations (kinesthetic modeling, drawing) are employed in several activities. Guided instruction that incorporates cues, questions, and advance organizers is provided to students at their level of readiness and learning pace, and students also have many opportunities for independent sense making.
- *Helping Students Extend and Apply Knowledge:* Students are encouraged to compare numbers and their corresponding number pairs to identify existing patterns. They use mathematical discourse and journal writing in the classroom to communicate their thinking and reasoning processes.

Common Core State Standards—Knowledge and Skills to Be Addressed

Standards for Mathematical Practice

MP2 Reason abstractly and quantitatively.

MP3 Construct viable arguments and critique the reasoning of others.

MP4 Model with mathematics.

MP5 Use appropriate tools strategically.

MP6 Attend to precision.

MP8 Look for and express regularity in repeated reasoning.

Standards for Mathematical Content

Domain: Operations and Algebraic Thinking

Cluster: Understand Addition as Putting Together and Adding to, and Understand Subtraction as Taking Apart and Taking From

K.OA.A.3 Decompose numbers less than or equal to 10 into pairs in more than one way, e.g., by using objects or drawings, and record each decomposition by a drawing or equation (e.g., 5 = 2 + 3 and 5 = 4 + 1).

Common Core State Standards—Prior Knowledge and Skills to Be Applied

Domain: Counting and Cardinality

Cluster: Know Number Names and the Count Sequence

K.CC.A.3 Write numbers from 0 to 20. Represent a number of objects with a written numeral 0–20 (with 0 representing a count of no objects).

Domain: Operations and Algebraic Thinking

Cluster: Understand Addition as Putting Together and Adding to, and Understand Subtraction as Taking Apart and Taking From

K.OA.A.1 Represent addition and subtraction with objects, fingers, mental images, drawings, sounds (e.g., claps), acting out situations, verbal explanations, expressions, or equations.

K.OA.A.2 Solve addition and subtraction word problems, and add and subtract within 10, e.g., by using objects or drawings to represent the problem.

Teacher's Lesson Summary

In this lesson, many components work together to help kindergarten students master the mathematics standard focused on decomposing numbers up to and including 10 into number pairs (K.OA.A.3). This is a critical standard for developing a strong foundation in number sense.

Because students need repeated exposure over time to acquire a solid conceptual understanding of this content, the lesson is designed to be presented as a series of mini-lessons conducted over many class sessions. It incorporates whole-group instruction, a guided instruction center where students work in a small (usually homogeneous) group with you, and a variety of math learning centers that facilitate mathematical discourse, communication, and practice; incorporate technology, games, nonlinguistic representation, reading and writing skills, science content related to animal behavior and habitat, and reflection; and provide students with the opportunity to work on several Standards for Mathematical Practice.

For the learning center activities, you will place students in small, differentiated groups based on your assessment of their readiness. These groups should be flexible—regularly adjusted based on formative assessment data. The lesson can be conducted with all of the centers described (five) or just a few.

Essential Question: How can grouping numbers help us solve problems?

Learning Objective: To find all number pairs for any given number, up to and including 10.

Knowledge/Vocabulary Objectives

At the conclusion of this lesson, students will understand that

• A number pair consists of two numbers that total another number.

• A number can be decomposed into pairs of numbers and in multiple ways.

Skill/Process Objectives

At the conclusion of this lesson, students will be able to

• Use objects to decompose numbers less than or equal to 10 into pairs and in multiple ways.

• Use drawings to decompose numbers less than or equal to 10 into pairs and in multiple ways.

• Record the decomposition of numbers less than or equal to 10 with a drawing.

• Record the decomposition of numbers less than or equal to 10 with an equation.

Resources/Preparation Needed

This lesson requires prior and ongoing preparation. In addition to setting up the various learning centers, labeling them, and stocking them with the appropriate materials (see the list that follows), you must set up and manage the student groups and prepare students for this kind of working arrangement. Make sure to plan how students will know when to rotate (e.g., an egg timer, an online stopwatch) and how you will communicate to students which center they will go to next. In addition, you will need to model each of the learning center activities to ensure students are familiar with the activity protocol.

- *For Class #1 and Center #1 (Guided Instruction):* Copies of the book *Math Fables*, written by Greg Tang and illustrated by Heather Cahoon (required text); one bag of manipulatives (sets of up to 10 counters, buttons, raisins, marbles, laminated animals to match the story, etc.) for each student; drawing paper and writing implements; traditional ten frame templates (available: http://lrt.ednet.ns.ca/PD/ BLM/table_of_contents.htm); precut lengths of yarn, approximately six inches long

- *For Center #2 (Independent Practice):* Additional copies of *Math Fables* and copies of *MATH-terpieces: The Art of Problem Solving* by Greg Tang and Greg Poprocki; an advance organizer (see **Figure A: Number Pair Recording Sheet**, p. 210); prepared sets of manipulatives in labeled plastic bags (e.g., 10 snap cubes, 9 counting bears, 8 counters, 7 marbles, 6 color tiles, etc.); drawing paper and implements

- *For Center #3 (Cooperative Learning Games):* A set of dominoes, spinners, dice, playing cards/ten frame cards, and the board game Shut the Box (optional)

- *For Center #4 (Reading and Writing):* Number and number pair cards; drawing paper and crayons/markers/colored pencils

- *For Center #5 (Technology):* Interactive whiteboard (optional); computer stations with Internet access

Activity Description to Share with Students

Numbers appear everywhere in our world. For example, we use numbers to count, to help us share things with our friends, to solve problems, and when playing games. This lesson will help you learn more about numbers and how a number can be broken apart into two different numbers or *number pairs*. Number pairs can be helpful to you in many ways. For example: Imagine you are playing a game with four of your friends. In this game, two players need to be in charge: one to spin the spinner and the other to keep score. How many people are left to play the game? If you know about number pairs, solving this problem will be easy.

During this lesson, you will work in a variety of mathematics centers. You will have time to work in a small group with the teacher, time to practice with other students, and time to practice on your own.

Lesson Activity Sequence—Class #1

Start the Lesson

1. Explain to students that they will be learning about *number pairs*. Post the learning objective and essential question, and discuss these with students so they will understand the goals for their learning.
2. Next, have a group of students sit in a horizontal row in front of the class. Lead the rest of the class in counting aloud the number of students sitting in the row. Then ask the student at the far left of the row to stand up while the other students remain seated.
3. Discuss these questions with the class: *How many students are standing? How many students are sitting? How many students are there in total?*
4. Explain the term *number pair* and the concept of using an addition sentence to represent the row of students (e.g., one student is standing and six students are sitting; $1 + 6 = 7$; 1 and 6 are a number pair for 7).
5. Next, have two students stand while the rest stay seated. Repeat the demonstration and questions process until you have illustrated all the number pairs that sum to the total number.
6. Tell students that today and over the next several days, they will be practicing finding number pairs. They will begin now by hearing a story that has number pairs in it.

Engaging Students in Learning the Content

1. Read the book *Math Fables* aloud to the class. While you read, pause regularly to ask probing questions to connect the stories to the learning objective. (Remind students to whisper their answers to your questions into their hands so that everyone has a chance to think about an answer and response; then call on individuals to provide responses.) Questions might include

- *How many total [raccoons] are there?*
- *What is the number pair described in the fable?*
- *What does the number pair total?*
- *Explain how you know the number pair [5, 2] has a total of [7]?*
- *Are there other number pairs with the same total?*

2. Still in the whole-group setting, ask small groups of students to stand up and act out various fables from the book. Start with the "Midnight Snack" fable. Assign five students to act out the part of the story's five raccoons. As you read through the fable, the five students will need to rearrange themselves to represent the various number pairs. Ask the rest of the class probing questions to monitor their developing understanding.

3. Continue with other fables until all students have had a chance to participate.

4. Give students time to practice working independently with the number pairs from the fables. Provide each with a bag of manipulatives containing some given number up to 10 (students struggling with the concepts should receive bags with fewer items). Ask students to think up their own "fable" and draw a picture to represent their story. They will need to use the manipulative provided as their total for their fable and find a number pair for that total. Observe students' work, providing corrective feedback and gathering formative data on individual students' developing understanding. Guide students who finish early to trade bags of manipulatives and create a second fable.

Close the Lesson

1. Ask the students: *What was the learning goal for today's lesson?* Have students turn to a partner to discuss the goal.

2. Ask volunteers to share their responses.

3. Tell students the concepts they learned today are very important and they will continue to work and play with number pairs in learning centers for several days. Describe each of the centers to the students, modeling various activities for students, as needed.

Lesson Activity Sequence—Classes #2–5: Small-Group Learning Centers

The five small-group learning centers are designed to work in conjunction with one another to cement students' mastery of the standard in multiple class sessions over a period of days or weeks. Your role is to provide guided practice, engage in continual formative assessment, and, eventually, move to a facilitator role as students continue to engage in practice experiences. As noted, student groupings should be planned but flexible, based on ongoing assessment and adjusted to reflect individuals' evolving understanding.

Note that the recommended time for kindergarten students to spend in each learning center is 10 to 15 minutes per session. The number of learning center sessions will vary with each class's progress toward mastery. In order to provide ongoing practice, various centers such as the Technology and Cooperative Learning Games centers might continue to include work with number pairs, while the Guided Instruction Center moves on to address other content and new learning objectives.

Start the Lesson

1. Refer to the posted learning objective and essential question, and discuss these with students. Have students explain in their own words what the learning objective means.
2. Place students into their assigned homogeneous groups for the day's first center rotation.
3. Remind students of the classroom procedures during the mathematics center times, including how, where, and when to rotate; behavioral expectations; the procedure for asking the teacher a question; and how to participate in a cooperative group. If you are introducing a new center activity, model its protocol expectations.

Engage Students in Learning the Content

Center #1: Guided Instruction

Provide direct, differentiated instruction in a small-group setting, adjusting your approach and the supports you use to suit student readiness.

ACTIVITY A: FINDING NUMBER PAIRS IN *MATH FABLES*

1. Choose another story from *Math Fables,* and explain to students that they will be modeling it, just as they did in the whole-group instructional activity. For example, if you select "Gone with the Wind," the students will use counters to model the fable's seven butterflies. Groups of students just beginning to master the concept might need to begin with a fable with a lower number, like four or five, which contain fewer number pairs.

2. Read the fable, pausing between each pair of numbers so students can arrange the two groups. Continue to ask probing questions, such as the following:

   • *Are there still seven butterflies all together when you have a group of two and a group of five?*

   • *What are all the different number pairs that would create a total of seven butterflies?*

   • *Explain or show how you know the number pair totals seven butterflies.*

3. Allow students to choose another fable to model. Use different manipulatives to represent each animal; for example, use raisins for "Antics" to represent the nine ants.

4. Now extend the learning by asking students to draw a picture of a number pair in the second fable. Below the drawing, ask students to write the corresponding numerals. For example, if a student draws a group of six and a group of one butterfly, the completed work might look like this:

$$6 \qquad + \qquad 1 \qquad = \qquad 7$$

Monitor students' progress, and ask them questions like these, in pairs or one on one:

   • *How many total butterflies are in your picture?*

   • *You and* [name of another student in the group] *have different groups of butterflies; do you both have a total of seven butterflies? Explain your thinking.*

   • *If the total is seven, does that mean if I add the two groups together the total will equal seven? How can we write that using symbols?*

5. Repeat this process with other fables: Students model groupings using manipulatives, record a grouping with a drawing, and then record that grouping with an equation.

ACTIVITY B: FINDING NUMBER PAIRS USING TEN FRAMES

1. Give each student a blank ten frame and 10 counters. The counters represent the animals in the various stories in *Math Fables*.
2. Choose a fable to model with the students—for example, "Gone with the Wind."
3. Read the fable, pausing between each pair of numbers. Prompt students to model the seven butterflies in "Gone with the Wind," using counters on their ten frames, as illustrated:

4. Distribute lengths of pre-cut yarn. Continue reading and have students model the number pairs using yarn to encircle each group on their card:

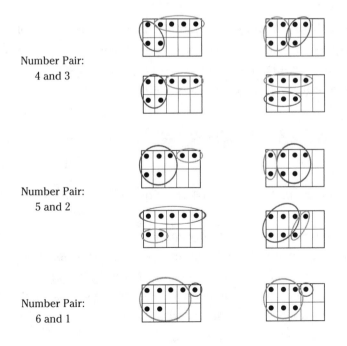

Number Pair:
4 and 3

Number Pair:
5 and 2

Number Pair:
6 and 1

5. Continue to use questioning to assess student understanding of number pairs and that there can be multiple number pairs to total a number.

6. Guide students to create a drawing and equation to represent the models they created with the ten frames. This step helps students move their thinking forward, from the concrete counters to representation (a drawing) and, eventually, to abstraction (if they are using numbers and symbols).

Center #2: Independent Practice

The Independent Practice Center's purpose is to extend the learning students build in the Guided Instruction center.

1. Students choose a fable from *Math Fables* or a page from *MATH-terpieces*. Students ready for an additional challenge can use the *MATH-terpieces* book to create a number triple rather than a number pair.

2. Students identify a number pair, model it (as needed) using prepared sets of manipulatives, record a drawing, and record an equation, using the **Number Pair Recording Sheet** (see **Figure A,** p. 210). Students who require additional scaffolding might be provided with a partially filled-in version of the Number Pair Recording Sheet, as illustrated:

Drawing	☆ ★	★ ★ ★	
Ten Frame	(ten frame with 2 dots)	(empty ten frame)	(empty ten frame)
Number	2		
Word	two		
Equation			

Center #3: Cooperative Learning/Game Table

This center should be set up with a multi-person game that reinforces the skills associated with the lesson objective. The following are a few sample games, but there are many resources available for game ideas that are easily accessible and free (see p. 209).

Game A: Domino Snake

- *Game Setup:* A spinner with numbers 1–10, a set of dominoes, a pair of 0–5 dice
- *Beginning-Level Procedure:* Player #1 spins the spinner and then finds a domino showing a pair that matches the number from the spin (e.g., a spin of 2 would mean finding a domino with two dots). The game moves on to the next player. On players' second spin, they look for a domino that reflects their spin *and* matches one of the numbers in the original domino's pair, forming a chain (see illustration). The first player with a Domino Snake that is six dominoes long is the winner.

- *Intermediate- and Advanced-Level Procedure:* Players use a pair of dice, rather than a spinner, to generate numbers, meaning they find the sum of the dice roll and use that number as they look for a domino.

Game B: 10's Go Fish

- *Game Setup:* Four complete sets of 1–10 ten frame cards
- *Procedure:* Spread the cards face down on a table. Each player chooses a predetermined number of cards (five is a good number for kindergarten students). Players take turns asking the other players for a number they could pair with one of their cards to make 10 (e.g., a player with a 9 card would ask, "Do you have any 1's?"). Once a player has no cards remaining, the game is over. The player with the most matches is the winner.
- *Modification:* Choose a number other than 10 (e.g., 9's Go Fish). This will require removing ten frame cards that are larger than the target number.

Game C: Shut the Box

- *Game Setup:* This is a classic number game. Game boards can be found at most local department stores and many online vendors.

- *Procedure:* Players roll two dice and, based on the sum, can "shut" various numbers in the box (e.g., if a player rolls a 3, then the 1 and 2 can be "shut" or just the 3). Detailed instructions can be found at www.ehow.com/how_8044927_shut-box-instructions.html

Center #4: Reading and Writing

The activities students engage in at this center will help to reinforce Mathematical Practice Standards 3 and 6, with a focus on mathematical communication and discourse. This center will also provide opportunities for students to do work connected to a variety of kindergarten ELA/literacy standards.

TASK A: STORY WRITING TO FIND THE TOTAL

Have a set of cards with number pairs making 10 written on them. Students choose a card and then create a story about the number pair, draw a picture to illustrate the story, and write an equation to represent the number pair and the total.

TASK B: STORY WRITING TO FIND A NUMBER PAIR

Have a set of seven cards, marked with the numerals 4–10. Students will choose a card and identify a corresponding number pair for the card chosen. Students will then create a story about the number pair, draw a picture to illustrate it, and write an equation to represent the number pair and the total. For students who are struggling, ask them to draw all the number pairs they can for a particular sum. They might use two different-colored crayons and use X's or dots to illustrate the pairs.

TASK C: CLASS JOURNAL

Display a prompt on a piece of posted chart paper or a whiteboard. If you have advanced readers, ask them to read the prompt to the group. If there is a group that struggles with reading and writing, read the prompt aloud, have a volunteer respond verbally, and model how that response could be recorded on the chart paper with words or drawings. Have students then respond independently to the prompt. Sample prompts include the following:

- *Today in math I learned* _____.
- *My favorite part of math today was* _____.
- *A number pair is* _____.

Center #5: Technology
This center can be used to reinforce the current learning objective and provide students with additional individualized practice/enrichment in other mathematical areas.

TASK A: COLLABORATIVE EQUATION GENERATION

- *Setup:* Place a given number of objects (any number 2–10) on an interactive white-board. (*Note:* If this technology is not available, this activity could be completed using magnets and a standard whiteboard.)
- *Procedure:* Students write the total number of objects on the screen. Next, they take turns dragging the objects into two groups to form a number pair and writing the number of objects in each group below the image. Then the entire small group collaborates to create a complete equation representing what is on screen, as shown:

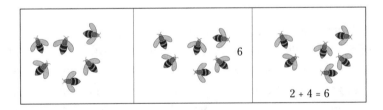

TASK B: INDEPENDENT INTERACTIVE GAMES

Students work on their own to access and play interactive games that reinforce the learning objective and provide corrective feedback.

- *Setup:* Desktop computers, laptops, mini-laptops, or tablets with an Internet connection and bookmarks to the designated games
- *Beginning Level:* Save the Whale (www.ictgames.com/10pipe.html) and Counting Bricks (http://primarygamesarena.com/Counting-bricks794)
- *Intermediate Level:* NCTM Ten Frame Game (http://illuminations.nctm.org/ActivityDetail.aspx?ID=75)
- *Intermediate/Advanced Level:* Math Limbo (www.gregtangmath.com)

Close the Lesson

"Wrap up" students' learning on a weekly basis, if not more frequently.

1. Read aloud the posted essential question and learning objective.
2. Engage the class in an activity that will allow you to informally assess student understanding. Here are some suggestions:
   - Review the "Class Journal" (see p. 207) with students. Ask volunteers to explain their journal response to the group.
   - Ask the students: *What was the learning goal for today's lesson?* Have students turn to a partner to talk about the prompt. Then have volunteers share their response.
   - Have students work in a collaborative group to create a number pair. Students can use physical objects to model the number pair. Have the students recite the corresponding equation.
   - Put a numeral (any number, 4–10) on the board for the class to see. Invite students to say a number pair for the number on the board until all pairs have been identified. Ask students if pairs in reverse order are the same (e.g., 4 and 1, 1 and 4). Have students explain their reasoning.

Additional Resources for This Lesson

Math for All Seasons: Mind Stretching Math Riddles by Greg Tang might be used in addition to the required texts, *Math Fables* and *MATH-terpieces,* as a source of extension activities.

Figure A | **Number Pair Recording Sheet**

Drawing	Ten Frame	Number	Word	Equation

Composing Two-Dimensional Shapes

Course: 1st grade Mathematics
Length of Lesson: Two hours; two 60-minute class periods

Introduction

In kindergarten, students learn to identify two- and three-dimensional shapes and begin to analyze and compare shapes by examining their attributes. Students also compose simple shapes to form larger shapes (e.g., they may form a square using two triangles or use two squares to form a rectangle). This learning forms a solid foundation for the geometry skills students will build in 1st grade.

The van Hiele Model of Geometric Thought, a theory that has been researched over several decades, describes how students learn geometry. The theory has influenced curriculum and instruction in the field of geometry, encouraging a focus on shapes and their characteristics in primary grade levels. In the Common Core standards, 1st grade students work on creating two- and three-dimensional composite shapes (e.g., students may form a square using two triangles or use two squares to form a rectangle). This marks the transition from what the van Hiele model identifies as the most basic, "level 0" geometric thinking (judging shapes by their appearance) to "level 1" thinking (seeing figures in terms of their components) (Fuys, Geddes, & Tischler, 1988). Students in 1st grade should be able to look at objects that exist in the world around them and identify two- or three-dimensional shapes that compose those objects. Mastering this lesson's objectives will improve students' spatial skills and help them make connections between their understanding of shapes and the world around them.

Strategies from the Framework for Instructional Planning

- *Creating the Environment for Learning:* The essential question and lesson objectives will be discussed with students throughout the lesson and placed in a visible location in the classroom. The first class session features formal cooperative learning, with students assigned specific roles and responsibilities within small groups. A literature and real-world connection will be used to help students make connections between the mathematical concepts and contextual situations. Throughout the lesson, students will receive feedback from peers, the teacher, and interactive technology.
- *Helping Students Develop Understanding:* The teacher will regularly use questioning techniques to develop and assess student understanding of the targeted mathematical concepts. Various manipulatives allow for nonlinguistic representation, and students will summarize their learning through whole-group discussion and in written responses in their math journals.
- *Helping Students Extend and Apply Knowledge:* Students will extend their knowledge by identifying similarities and differences when looking for patterns as they create two-dimensional composite figures. They will generate and test hypotheses as they use their spatial reasoning skills to manipulate the shapes into the proper locations within composite figures and by composing figures with tangrams.

Common Core State Standards—Knowledge and Skills to Be Addressed

Standards for Mathematical Practice

MP1 Make sense of problems and persevere in solving them.

MP4 Model with mathematics.

MP7 Look for and make use of structure.

Standards for Mathematical Content
Domain: Geometry

Cluster: Reason with Shapes and Their Attributes

1.G.A.2 Compose two-dimensional shapes (rectangles, squares, trapezoids, triangles, half-circles, and quarter-circles) or three-dimensional shapes (cubes, right rectangular prisms, right circular cones, and right circular cylinders) to create a composite shape, and compose new shapes from the composite shape.

Common Core State Standards—Prior Knowledge and Skills to Be Applied
Domain: Geometry

Cluster: Identify and Describe Shapes (Squares, Circles, Triangles, Rectangles, Hexagons, Cubes, Cones, Cylinders, and Spheres)

K.G.A.2 Correctly name shapes regardless of their orientations and overall size.

Cluster: Analyze, Compare, Create, and Compose Shapes

K.G.B.6 Compose simple shapes to form larger shapes.

Cluster: Reason with Shapes and Their Attributes

1.G.A.1 Distinguish between defining attributes (e.g., triangles are closed and three-sided) versus non-defining attributes (e.g., color, orientation, overall size); build and draw shapes to possess defining attributes.

Teacher's Lesson Summary

This lesson emphasizes the two-dimensional component of Standard 1.G.A.2, and engages students in creating composite shapes and composing figures using those composite shapes.

The lesson is structured to combine whole-class instruction with small-group instruction in three rotations: Guided Instruction, Cooperative Learning, and Independent Practice. The small-group structure will allow you to differentiate the learning based on student readiness. You can modify the guided instruction to meet the needs of each small group. Note that success with the independent practice and cooperative learning activities is not reliant on information presented during the Guided Instruction Rotation. This means all three rotations can run simultaneously; the order in which students complete the rotations will not affect achievement.

The skills introduced and developed during this lesson are key to strong spatial reasoning. During the lesson, students will have multiple opportunities to engage in hands-on learning, using a variety of manipulatives and technology. Tangram puzzles, the focus of Class #2 (see p. 219), are an engaging way to provide ongoing practice with shape composition. These ancient puzzles consist of a square that is cut into seven shapes—two large triangles, a medium triangle, two small triangles, a square, and a parallelogram, with the puzzle solver challenged to use these seven shapes to compose an image—traditionally, various animal and human figures. Tangram puzzles and work with pattern blocks can be incorporated during times that are not specific to math and without direct teacher instruction to reinforce the mathematical concepts and skills.

Essential Question: How can shapes be used to create other shapes and objects we see in our world?

Learning Objective: To use two-dimensional shapes to create composite shapes.

Knowledge/Vocabulary Objectives

At the conclusion of this lesson, students will understand that

• A shape can be composed of various different shapes.

• Objects in our world are composed of different shapes.

Skill/Process Objective

At the conclusion of this lesson, students will be able to

• Create a composite shape from two-dimensional shapes.

Resources/Preparation Needed

• Sets of shape matching cards cut from the **Matching Shapes Activity Resource** (see **Figure A,** p. 224), shuffled and packed in plastic baggies, one per student; pattern blocks

• *Grandfather Tang's Story* by Ann Tompert (for alternatives, see Additional Resources for This Lesson, pp. 222–223)

• Various printed tangram puzzles (see Additional Resources for This Lesson)

• *For the Guided Instruction Rotation:* Fraction circles or pre-cut fraction circles (whole, halves, quarters), one set per student

- *For the Cooperative Learning Rotation:* the **Composing Shapes Cooperative Learning Activity Resource** (see **Figure B,** p. 225), one per group; precut pattern blocks and a glue stick, one per group (pattern block stickers could also be used)
- *For the Independent Practice Rotation:* Computer stations with Internet access, with browsers open to the Patch Tool from the NCTM Illuminations website: http://illuminations.nctm.org/ActivityDetail.aspx?ID=27

Activity Description to Share with Students

When you look at the world around you, you will see shapes everywhere. Most of the objects you see are a combination of these different shapes. Throughout this lesson, we will practice identifying the shapes in everyday objects. You will also get to play with shapes: use them to solve puzzles and to create new shapes that reflect what you see in the world and in your imagination.

Lesson Activity Sequence—Class #1

Start the Lesson

1. Post and discuss the essential question, learning objective, and lesson objectives.
2. Activate students' prior knowledge with a shape-matching activity. Distribute card sets cut from the **Matching Shapes Activity Resource** (see **Figure A,** p. 224). Ask students to work independently to match each shape card with its corresponding name card and "sides" card. Give students about five minutes to complete the task.
3. As students work, walk around the classroom, informally assessing students' knowledge through observation and questioning.

Engage Students in Learning the Content

Whole-Group Learning and Discussion

1. Distribute sets of pattern blocks, and display the picture in Example A. (Begin by displaying the composite shape with each individual shape in a different color for students to easily recognize the shapes that make up the composite shape. To make this activity more challenging, use images that display all shapes in the same color.) Ask the following questions:

- *What does this picture remind you of?*
- *What shapes do you see in the picture?*
- *What other shapes could you use to create the same picture?*

As you question students, give them time to experiment with their pattern blocks.

Example A

2. Display the picture in Example B and ask the students to turn to a partner and discuss the same three questions:

Example B

- *What does this shape remind you of?*
- *What shapes do you see in the picture?*
- *What other shapes could you use to create the same picture?*

Listen in on the partner discussions to identify points of confusion or misconceptions.

3. After about one minute of partner discussion time, ask students to share their answers. Be sure to clarify any misconceptions you noted during observations.

Small-Group Rotations/Independent Practice

Place students in small, heterogeneous groups, and explain their group assignments. Each rotation should last approximately 15 minutes to allow time for students to visit all three rotations.

Guided Instruction Rotation

In the Guided Instruction Rotation, you will facilitate learning with a small group of students.

1. Begin by discussing with students the meaning of a composite shape.
2. Tell students that they will use shapes such as circles, triangles, squares, hexagons, and so on to *compose* new shapes or pictures.
3. Give each student a set of fraction circles including a whole, two halves, and four quarters.
4. Ask students to find the whole circle.
5. Have students cover their whole circle using other pieces. Once they have done so, point out to all students the different ways in which the circle was composed. If there were any ways that weren't used, ask students if they can think of other ways to compose the circle.

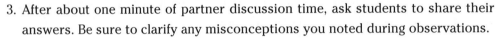

6. Ask students in what ways they could compose a half circle. The vocabulary terms *half*, *fourth*, and *quarter* can be used incidentally here (e.g., "The half circle could be composed of one half or two quarters"), but these terms should be formally introduced as the focus of direct vocabulary instruction in future 1st grade lessons.

7. Have students explore the concept of composing shapes out of previous compositions. Begin by asking the students to create the compositions in Example C:

Example C

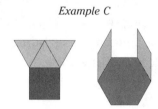

8. Once students have created the composed shapes, explain that they will need to use each of these to create the next composition, Example D:

Example D

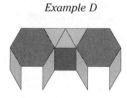

9. Give students a few minutes to compose their own shapes. If time allows, check in with the students working in the Cooperative Learning and Independent Practice rotations.

10. Ask students to compose new shapes out of their previous compositions.

COOPERATIVE LEARNING ROTATION

1. Explain to students that they will be working in a team of two (or three, as necessary). Within the teams, students will assume the roles of Recorder, Shape Manipulator, and (if there are three) Controller.

2. Give teams a trapezoid and a hexagon pattern block as well as a baggie containing several of each of the different types of pattern blocks. Ask students to use the pattern blocks to find all the different compositions of the trapezoid and the hexagon. The Recorder will draw the shapes on the **Composing Shapes Cooperative Learning Activity Resource** (see **Figure B**, p. 225); the Shape Manipulator will manipulate the pre-cut pattern blocks; and the Controller will check the work of both the Recorder and the Shape Manipulator. Finally, the Recorder will use a glue stick to paste each "checked" shape onto the recording sheet. Students will take turns performing each role.

3. Collect the completed recording sheets at the end of the rotation, and review the students' work to assess for understanding. During Class #2, students will have a chance to revisit and reflect on this work.

INDEPENDENT PRACTICE ROTATION

The Independent Practice Rotation will consist of one or both of the following tasks.

- *Task A.* Students will use pattern block manipulatives or pre-cut pattern blocks and glue to compose any design or picture they like. It can be something they have seen in the world or something that they imagine. If students use manipulatives, take a digital photo of their design to preserve it. When explaining the task, display sample student designs, like the ones shown, to help students understand what they will be doing.

Example E

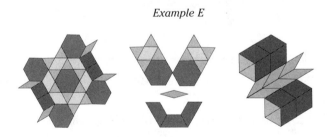

- *Task B.* Set up computer stations and have the Patch Tool from the NCTM Illuminations website open. Students will use virtual pattern blocks to create a design, choosing from the various picture models provided. The Patch Tool allows for easy task differentiation; you can opt to set it up to display each picture as an outline only (for greater challenge) or with the individual shapes within the outline showing (for supportive scaffolding). Students might also use the Patch Tool to create their own unique designs or pictures.

Close the Lesson

1. Remind students of the learning and lesson objectives. Ask students to show a thumbs-up if they feel they understand the learning for the day or a thumbs down if they still have questions.
2. Display the following sentence starters, and ask students to choose a sentence to complete in their math journal:
   - *Today I learned that shapes can be used to* _____.
   - *One thing new that I learned today is* _____.
   - *The part I liked best about today's math lesson was* _____ *because*
   _____.
   - *I still have a question about* _____.
3. Review student journals prior to the next math session to help inform your instruction based on student journal responses and levels of comprehension.

Lesson Activity Sequence—Class #2

Start the Lesson

1. Ask student volunteers to share what they learned in the previous lesson.
2. Remind students of the learning and lesson objectives.
3. Distribute pattern blocks, and post an image of the yellow hexagon that students examined during the Cooperative Learning Rotation:

Ask students to compose the yellow hexagon pattern block using four shapes. Ask students if this hexagon could be composed of five shapes. Six shapes? Seven shapes?

4. Ask students how many different ways they think this hexagon could be composed. Be sure to clarify that each "way" consists of a certain number and type of shapes, rather than the particular pattern of those shapes. For example, the following compositions (one blue rhombus, one green triangle, and one red trapezoid) count as a single way of composing the hexagon.

Have students share their thoughts with a partner.

5. Call on volunteers to share their ideas with the rest of the class. Create a chart, as illustrated, to keep track of the seven different possible shape compositions.

Composing a Hexagon Pattern Block			
Red Trapezoid	Blue Rhombus	Green Triangle	COMPOSITION
2	0	0	
1	1	1	
1	0	?	?

Engage Students in Learning the Content

1. Explain to students that today, they will learn how to use tangrams to compose shapes. Ask students if they are familiar with the term *tangrams* and, if so, to describe what a tangram is. (*Note:* Most students will be unfamiliar with the term.)

2. Announce that you will now be reading a story that will explain tangrams and how they can be used to compose shapes. Read the book *Grandfather Tang's Story* by Ann Tompert or *Three Pigs, One Wolf, Seven Magic Shapes* by Grace Maccarone.

3. At the conclusion of the story ask students to share what they learned. Ask questions such as
   * *What is a tangram?*
   * *Where did it come from?*
   * *What is a tangram used for?*
   * *Is there anything special about the shapes of the tangram?*

4. Display a tangram puzzle (in outline only, not with individual shapes outlined) for the class to complete as a whole. Prompt students to explain what shape they might choose first and why. Use a think-aloud strategy to talk students through a rational method for composing the picture using all seven tangram pieces with no gaps or overlaps of the pieces (e.g., try to place the large triangles in the largest space first).

5. If additional practice seems necessary, complete a second puzzle as a whole class, repeating the think-aloud approach.

6. Distribute a variety of printed tangram puzzles, some showing the individual tangram pieces outlined and some that do not, as illustrated:

7. Have students choose a puzzle to compose independently. Most should begin with puzzles in which each individual tangram shape is outlined.

8. Once students have mastered these puzzles (it may be many sessions before they reach this point), ask them to try a puzzle in which the picture is outlined but not the individual shapes. This will be much more challenging, and many students will need guidance.

9. While students are working on their puzzles, you might ask some students to work with virtual tangrams from the National Library of Virtual Manipulatives Tangrams application, available online (see Additional Resources for This Lesson, p. 223).

10. For students who exhibit mastery at composing the pictures using tangrams, propose a challenge by having them create a square using all seven tangram pieces.

Close the Lesson

1. Engage students in a Shape Walk to reflect on their learning and make connections. As a class, take a walk throughout the school building, outside, or around the classroom. Distribute note cards and pencils, and instruct students to look for objects that are composed of more than one shape. Have students record their observations on their note card.

2. Once the walk is completed, return to the classroom to discuss the student observations. Facilitate the discussion using questions such as these:
   - *How can shapes be used to create the objects we see in our world?*
   - *What objects did you observe that were composite shapes?*
   - *What shapes composed the objects you observed?*
   - *Can you think of any jobs that might need to use shapes to compose objects?*

3. If time allows, have students work independently to compose one or more of the objects they observed, using their choice of tangrams or pattern blocks. Observe their work and provide feedback.

Additional Resources for This Lesson

More information on tangrams can be found at www.cleavebooks.co.uk/trol/trolxk. pdf. See the following online resources for materials to use in this lesson or for activities to reinforce learning:

- Dynamic Paper (use to create printable pattern blocks): http://illuminations. nctm.org/ActivityDetail.aspx?ID=205

- Virtual Pattern Blocks: http://nlvm.usu.edu/en/nav/frames_asid_169_g_1_t_3. html
- Virtual Tangrams: http://nlvm.usu.edu/en/nav/frames_asid_268_g_1_t_3.html
- Printable Seven Piece Tangram: http://figur8.net/baby/2011/03/01/right-brain-education-tangrams/
- Tangram Printable Puzzles: http://etc.usf.edu/clipart/galleries/math/tangram_outline_puzzles.php
- National Library of Virtual Manipulatives Tangrams application: http://nlvm.usu.edu/en/nav/frames_asid_268_g_1_t_3.html

The following books provide a literature connection to this lesson's content and might be used in addition to or in place of the required text, *Grandfather Tang's Story*:

- *A Cloak for the Dreamer* by Aileen Friedman
- *Three Pigs, One Wolf, Seven Magic Shapes* by Grace Maccarone

Figure A | **Matching Shapes Activity Resource**

Shape Cards	*Name Cards*	*Sides Cards*
	Square	4 sides
	Rectangle	4 sides
	Triangle	3 sides
	Trapezoid	4 sides
	Hexagon	6 sides

Figure B | **Composing Shapes Cooperative Learning Activity Resource**

Names: **Date:**

Student Roles: Recorder   Shape Manipulator   Controller

Problem #1

Use 2 shapes to create a ⬯ . Paste in your work here.

Use 3 shapes to create a ⬯ . Paste in your work here.

Show some other ways you could create a ⬯ .

How many different ways do you think there are to create a ⬯ ?

Problem #2

Use 2 shapes to create a ⬡. Paste in your work here.

Use 3 shapes to create a ⬡. Paste in your work here.

Use 4 shapes to create a ⬡. Paste in your work here.

Show other ways you could create a ⬡.

How many different ways do you think there are to create a ⬡?

Collecting and Representing Measurement Data

Course: 2nd grade Mathematics
Length of Lesson: One hour; one 60-minute class period plus ongoing project time

Introduction

In kindergarten and 1st grade, students learn about measurement with nonstandard units. They compare lengths of various objects and focus on understanding the process of length measurement. In 2nd grade, students build on these prior experiences, which include knowing how to select and use appropriate measurement tools and measurement units including inches, feet, centimeters, and meters.

This lesson focuses on supporting students as they encounter largely unfamiliar concepts required in the 2nd grade Measurement and Data domain of the Common Core standards. Not only are the Common Core's standards for measurement more complex and rigorous in 2nd grade than they are in the prior primary grade levels, but students will also be expected to represent measurement data using a line plot.

Strategies from the Framework for Instructional Planning

- *Creating the Environment for Learning:* The essential question and learning objective will be discussed with students throughout the lesson and placed in a visible location in the classroom. Students will be prompted to personalize the learning objective at the beginning of the lesson, and feed-back will be provided throughout the lesson by peers, the teacher, and optional interactive technology. Real-world data will be used to engage students and help them make connections between the mathematical concepts and contextual situations. Formal cooperative learning will occur during Class #1 of the lesson, with students assigned roles within their pairs.

- *Helping Students Develop Understanding:* The teacher will use cues, questions, and advance organizers at various stages of the lesson. Nonlinguistic representation will be heavily emphasized when activating prior knowledge and through the direct vocabulary instruction of the term *line plot.* Students will engage in multiple practice opportunities designed to help them improve both their measurement skills and their skill at representing data on a line plot.

- *Helping Students Extend and Apply Knowledge:* Students will extend their knowledge through the use of the ongoing measurement project described in the lesson. They will make predictions about the change in plant height and pencil length over time, and they will test their predictions by recording daily measurements and looking for patterns in the measurement data they collect.

Common Core State Standards—Knowledge and Skills to Be Addressed

Standards for Mathematical Practice

MP5 Use appropriate tools strategically.

MP6 Attend to precision.

MP7 Look for and make use of structure.

Standards for Mathematical Content

Domain: Measurement and Data

Cluster: Represent and Interpret Data

2.MD.D.9 Generate measurement data by measuring lengths of several objects to the nearest whole unit, or by making repeated measurements of the same object. Show the measurements by making a line plot, where the horizontal scale is marked off in whole-number units.

Common Core State Standards—Prior Knowledge and Skills to Be Applied

Domain: Measurement and Data

Cluster: Measure and Estimate Lengths in Standard Units

2.MD.A.1 Measure the length of an object by selecting and using appropriate tools such as rulers, yardsticks, meter sticks, and measuring tapes.

2.MD.A.2 Measure the length of an object twice, using length units of different lengths for the two measurements; describe how the two measurements relate to the size of the chosen unit.

Cluster: Represent and Interpret Data

1.MD.C.4 Organize, represent, and interpret data with up to three categories; ask and answer questions about the total number of data points, how many in each category, and how many more or less are in one category than in another.

Teacher's Lesson Summary

This lesson emphasizes the connection from 2nd grade students' prior knowledge of measurement, including how to select and use appropriate measurement tools and units, to the unfamiliar concept of representing measurement data using a line plot. You will provide students opportunities to practice measuring skills and use tables and line plots to record real-world data—most notably, the increasing height of plants grown in the classroom and the decreasing length of pencils as they are used and sharpened, both of which students will track in this lesson's ongoing project component. The project as described takes place over the course of a calendar month, but it could be extended to provide additional practice on the focus skills or to incorporate the identification of growth or deterioration patterns. The time required each day for measurement and recording should be minimal and could be integrated into a daily classroom routine. If it is not possible to grow plants in the classroom, the Growing Plants Gizmo by ExploreLearning.com could be used to simulate plant growth.

Essential Question: How can measurement data be recorded and represented?

Learning Objective: To use line plots to record and represent measurement data.

Knowledge/Vocabulary Objective

At the conclusion of this lesson, students will understand that

- A line plot is a way to capture and organize data.

Skill/Process Objectives

At the conclusion of this lesson, students will be able to

- Select appropriate measuring tools and units.
- Measure objects to the nearest whole unit (inches, feet, centimeter, meter).
- Use a line plot, marked in whole units, to represent collected measurement data.

Resources/Preparation Needed

- Online access to the PBS Kids video "On the Right Track," streaming at http:// pbskids.org/go/
- A prepared set of number lines that students can use to practice plotting data (see the **Line Plot Resource, Figure A,** p. 238), one per student
- Measurement tools, including rulers, yardsticks, meter sticks, and tape measures
- A handout to guide students' in-class measurement activity (see the **Collecting Measurement Data Resource, Figure B,** p. 239), one per student
- A graphic organizer to support vocabulary development (see the **Verbal/Visual Word Association Resource, Figure C,** p. 241), one per student
- A handout to guide students' work on the ongoing measurement project (see the **Measurement Project Resource, Figure D,** p. 242), one per student
- Disposable cups filled with soil, plant seedlings, and unsharpened pencils—one of each, per student
- Masking tape to label cups and pencils
- Chart or butcher paper to create class line plots documenting the project data

Activity Description to Share with Students

Measurement is a skill that you will use throughout your life to help you understand the size of objects and spaces. You will get your height and weight measured when you go to the doctor. You will see distances measured on roads and on sports fields. Carpenters need precise measurements when constructing furniture and building homes. Movers need to be able to estimate measurements to be sure furniture will fit through doors. Designers need to be able to make precise measurements when cutting fabric and sewing clothing. This lesson will provide opportunities for you to master your measurement skills. It will also teach you how to use a line plot to record and represent measurement data in a way that will help you understand and use it.

Lesson Activity Sequence—Class #1

Start the Lesson

1 Post and discuss the essential question and learning objective.
2. Remind students that they have had many prior experiences with measurement and they have learned to use various tools and units of measure. Today's lesson will build upon those experiences and teach them how to organize a set of measurement data.
3. Give students the opportunity to personalize the learning objective by asking them to respond in writing to the following question: *When might you need to collect multiple measurements and record the data?*
4. Show the PBS Kids video titled "On the Right Track" to activate students' background knowledge.
5. Engage students in a class discussion about what they already know about length and measurement. Use a graphic organizer to record the discussion, as illustrated below:

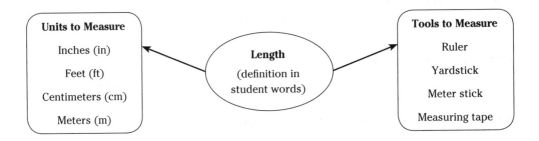

Be sure that students can state the definition of *length* in their own words and describe the various measurement tools and units that they have used previously.

6. Ask student volunteers to explain when they would measure objects using inches (rather than feet) and centimeters (rather than meters). Also prompt students to explain when and why they might use each of the various measurement tools (e.g., "I would measure the height of a door with a tape measure because a ruler would be too small").

Engage Students in Learning the Content

1. Explain to students that one of the learning objectives is to "understand that a line plot can be used to organize data."
2. Ask students how they have seen data displayed in the past (e.g., tally chart, pictograph, bar graph).
3. Display a sample line plot (see below) and ask for volunteers to describe what they think the line plot represents.

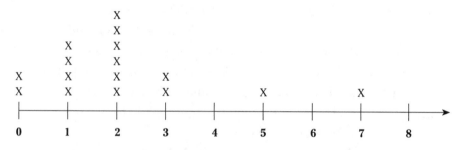

Mrs. Olson's 2nd Grade Class: Number of Siblings

Questions might include the following:

- *What is the most common number of siblings of students in Mrs. Olson's class?*
- *What other numbers of siblings are common to students in Mrs. Olson's class?*
- *What numbers of siblings are least common to students in Mrs. Olson's class?*
- *How many students are in Mrs. Olson's class?*
- *How many students have an odd number of siblings?*
- *How many students have an even number of siblings?*
- *Is there any other information you can gain from the line plot?*

4. Explain that sometimes a line plot is also called a *dot plot*—this is because dots can be used to represent the data points or other marks. Be sure students understand the following concepts:
   - A line plot is a number line and can represent an infinite number of values.
   - A line plot can be used to represent all kinds of data (measurement data in this lesson).
   - Each mark on a line plot represents one data point.
   - A line plot needs to be long enough to capture all the values you want to capture (e.g., when plotting students' birthday months, the line would need to extend to the number 12).
   - A line plot can be a quick visual to identify the most occurring and least occurring data points.

5. Next, provide data to students so they can practice creating their own line plot. When possible, use previously collected class or school data (e.g., "Shoe Sizes of Students in Our Class," "Month of Birth of Students in Our Class") to promote engagement and provide real-world context.

6. Ask students what values their number line needs to include, and then have them justify their reasoning (e.g., "My number line for the month of birth line plot will need to include numbers up through 12 because there are 12 months students could be born in").

7. Distribute the **Line Plot Resource** (see **Figure A,** p. 238), which is a set of number lines for students to use to plot data. Be sure to review this handout with students, as not all markings are labeled, and some may find it confusing. Allow them to practice plotting data, and observe their work, providing corrective feedback.

8. Bring the class back together and show students five objects in the classroom that they will measure. (Decide on these objects ahead of time; they should be easily measured using both inches and feet. Suggestions include a student desk top, classroom window height, a tissue box, classroom door width, classroom shelf height/width, and textbook length/width.)

9. Randomly assign students to groups of four. Within their groups, allow students to choose a partner, and then assign each pair a measuring unit: either inches or feet. Distribute the **Collecting Measurement Data Resource** (see **Figure B,** p. 239), and go over the work they will be doing:

- The pairs will measure all five objects, using their assigned unit of measure; record their measurements on the resource handout; and display the measurements on a line plot. Students will rotate between the roles of Measurer, the person who will select the tool and measure the object, and Recorder, the person who will record the measurement using the appropriate unit.

- Once the measurements have been completed, the pairs will compare their line plots with each other and draw conclusions based on their data. The resource handout prompts students to look for similarities and differences between one another's work and provide peer feedback.

- The groups will also be prompted to discuss and come to an agreement on the questions in Part 3 of the handout.

Anticipate that students will need support and feedback as they work. Lead them to the understanding that the two line plots generated within their group are similar (they all have five data points) but different in that the points lie at different values because the pairs used different units when measuring the objects. Students should come to realize that the same object can be the same size but have different values of measure, depending on the unit used to measure the object. Students may also notice that they have more repeat values for the feet unit because they have to round to the nearest whole when measuring (e.g., a 14-inch measure on a line plot would be 1 foot when using the feet unit). Collect this handout and use it as informal assessment data about individual student progress toward mastery.

Close the Lesson

1. To summarize their learning for the day, have students work to complete the **Verbal/Visual Word Association Resource** (see **Figure C,** p. 241). Be prepared to provide feedback and support to students as they complete their organizers. Here is an example of a completed organizer:

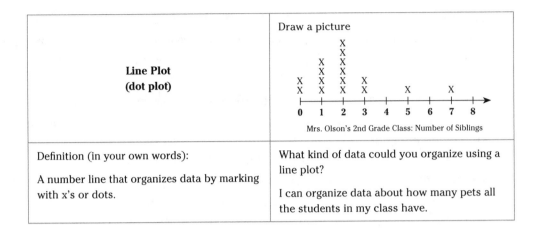

Line Plot (dot plot)	Draw a picture
Definition (in your own words): A number line that organizes data by marking with x's or dots.	**What kind of data could you organize using a line plot?** I can organize data about how many pets all the students in my class have.

2. Remind students of the learning objectives and the personalized objective they wrote at the beginning of class.

3. Have students write a 3, a 2, or a 1 on a sticky note to represent their understanding of the learning objectives for the day and place the sticky note on the board, wall, or teacher's desk. (A 3 would represent complete understanding, a 2 would represent partial understanding, and a 1 would represent limited understanding.) Although student names are not on the sticky notes, you will be able to see collectively where students self-assess themselves. If the majority of students are a 3, for example, then you would know that most students feel they have a complete understanding of the concept. The completed Line Plot Resource (see Figure A) can provide deeper insight into individual student mastery.

Ongoing Measurement Project

Start the Project—Day 1

1. Remind students of the previous day's learning objectives, and explain that they will be participating in a project that will allow them to further their mastery of those learning objectives.

2. Ask students to names objects that *grow* or *shrink* over time (e.g., plant height, human height, human weight, tire tread), and create a class list of these ideas on the board.

3. Tell students that they will each receive a seed/seedling to plant in a cup and an unsharpened pencil. Explain to students that over the next month, they will be collecting their own data on their plant height and pencil length. They will be responsible for watering their seedling regularly and sharpening and using their pencil regularly. They will also be responsible for monitoring the growth or deterioration of each item over time and capturing data about growth or deterioration.

4. Give each student a copy of the **Measurement Project Resource** (see **Figure D,** pp. 242–244) and have them predict what will happen to the plant height over time and the pencil length over time.

5. Use a piece of masking tape to label each student's seedling cup and pencil. Give each student his or her own cup of soil and seedling to plant and water, then place these seedlings in a sunny spot.

6. Discuss with students what appropriate measurement units might be for measuring both the plant and the pencil length. (*Note:* We suggest that the plant be measured using centimeters and the pencil, using inches. Students need to make all measurements within each project in the same unit in order to complete the whole-class line plots.)

7. Discuss how often the plant and the pencil should be measured and why. (*Note:* We suggest that the plant be measured less frequently than the pencil, as the growth will take more time to notice. Measuring the plant weekly and the pencil daily may be the best option; the Measurement Project Resource reflects this approach.)

8. Explain to students that they will record their individual measurements using the Measurement Project Resource and also display their results on whole-class line plots. (*Note:* You will need to create a whole-class line plot for each week that the plants are measured and a whole-class line plot for each day that the pencils are measured. For example:

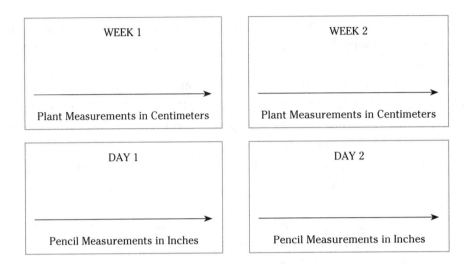

Post the line plots in the classroom at a height that students can reach to record their data.)

Engage Students in the Project—Days 1–20

1. Have students use an appropriate tool to measure their plant height and pencil length.
2. Students should record their weekly/daily measurements in the tables and line plots on their Measurement Project Resource sheet and on the whole-class line plots posted in the classroom. (*Note:* After the initial measurements, students should sharpen their pencils and use them regularly. Students should be given time to water their plants regularly.)

Close the Project—Day 20

1. Use the whole-class line plots for the plants and pencils to facilitate a whole-class discussion about what the data show.

   Questions to consider include
   - *How did the plant data change over time? How do you know?*
   - *How did the pencil data change over time? How do you know?*
   - *How does the class data set compare to your individual data?*

- *Did anything surprise you about the data?*
- *Is there another way we could represent the data in one chart or graph that would allow us to see the change in the data over time? (e.g., a line graph)*

2. Ask students to analyze their own data to look for any patterns over time and determine if their original prediction was correct.

3. Have students summarize their learning on their Measurement Project Resource sheet.

Additional Resources for This Lesson

See the following online resources for activities to reinforce learning:

- BrainPOPJr (www.brainpopjr.com/math/measurement/inchesandfeet/) features an Activity Page providing practice measuring objects in paper clips, inches, and centimeters and a Game Page providing practice selecting appropriate tools and units.
- Plop It! (www.shodor.org/interactivate/activities/PlopIt/) is an interactive line plot tool.
- Interactive Dot Plot (www.cengage.com/statistics/book_content/0495389536_mendenhall/applets/dotHow.html) provides practice plotting data and immediate feedback.

The following books provide a literature connection to this lesson's content:

- *Length* by Henry Pluckrose
- *How Big Is a Foot?* by Rolf Myller

Figure A | **Line Plot Resource**

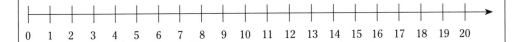

Figure B | **Collecting Measurement Data Resource**

My Name: _____   My Partner's Name: _____

Also in Our Group: _____   Date: _____

Part 1

Work with your partner to collect measurements for the five objects identified by your teacher. Use the unit assigned to your pair. Record your data in the table below, and use a checkmark to show the role you performed for each measurement.

Item	Measurement (include unit of measure)	I was the Measurer	I was the Recorder

Part 2

Work independently to represent your data on the line plot.

0   5   10   15   20   25   30   35   40   45

(continued)

Figure B | **Collecting Measurement Data Resource (*continued*)**

Part 3

Work in your group of four to compare your line plots and answer the following questions.

1. One of the line plots represents measurements in inches and the other represents measurements in feet. What do you notice that is the same about the two line plots?

2. What do you notice that is different about the two line plots?

3. Based on your comparisons, what conclusion can you draw about the units of measure, inches and feet?

4. Are the measurement values grouped differently when you compare the inch line plot to the feet line plot? If so, why do you think this is?

	Draw a picture
Line Plot **(dot plot)**	
Definition (in your own words):	What kind of data could you organize using a line plot?

Figure C | **Verbal/Visual Word Association Resource**

Figure D | **Measurement Project Resource**

My Name: _____

Plant Height

Predict what you think will happen to the plant height over time.

What unit of measure will you use to measure the height of your plant?

Use the table to record weekly data for the height of your plant.

Date	Measure

Use the line plots to represent your weekly measurement data.

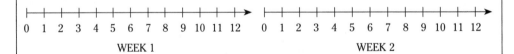

```
├─┼─┼─┼─┼─┼─┼─┼─┼─┼─┼─┼─►   ├─┼─┼─┼─┼─┼─┼─┼─┼─┼─┼─┼─►
0  1  2  3  4  5  6  7  8  9 10 11 12    0  1  2  3  4  5  6  7  8  9 10 11 12
           WEEK 1                                    WEEK 2
```

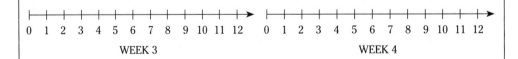

```
├─┼─┼─┼─┼─┼─┼─┼─┼─┼─┼─┼─►   ├─┼─┼─┼─┼─┼─┼─┼─┼─┼─┼─┼─►
0  1  2  3  4  5  6  7  8  9 10 11 12    0  1  2  3  4  5  6  7  8  9 10 11 12
           WEEK 3                                    WEEK 4
```

Explain what happened to the height of the plant over time and if your prediction was correct.

Figure D | **Measurement Project Resource (*continued*)**

Pencil Length

Predict what you think will happen to the pencil length over time.

What unit of measure will you use to measure the length of your pencil?

	Date	Measure
Use the table to record daily data for the length of your pencil.		

Use the line plots to represent your daily measurement data.

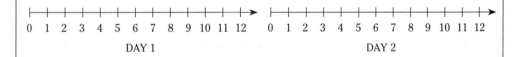

0 1 2 3 4 5 6 7 8 9 10 11 12   0 1 2 3 4 5 6 7 8 9 10 11 12
                DAY 1   DAY 2

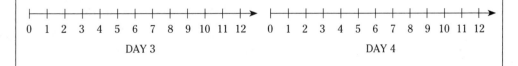

0 1 2 3 4 5 6 7 8 9 10 11 12   0 1 2 3 4 5 6 7 8 9 10 11 12
                DAY 3   DAY 4

(*continued*)

Figure D | **Measurement Project Resource (*continued*)**

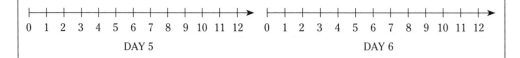

DAY 5   DAY 6

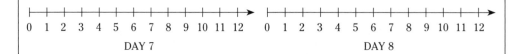

DAY 7   DAY 8

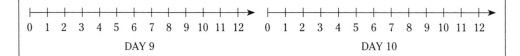

DAY 9   DAY 10

Explain what happened to the height of the plant over time and if your prediction was correct.

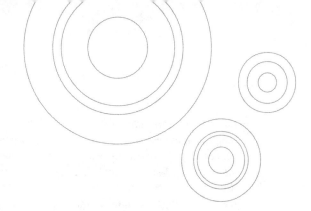

References

Baroody, A. J., & Benson, A. P. (2001). Early number instruction. *Teaching Children Mathematics, 8,* 154–158.

Byrne, B. (1998). *The foundation of literacy: The child's acquisition of the alphabetic principle.* Hove, UK: Psychology Press.

Clements, D. H., & Sarama, J. (2009). *Learning and teaching early math: The learning trajectories approach.* New York: Routledge.

Coleman, D., & Pimentel, S. (2012, May 16). *Revised publishers' criteria for the Common Core State Standards in English language arts and literacy, grades K–2.* Retrieved from http://www.corestandards.org/assets/Publishers_Criteria_for_K-2.pdf

Common Core Standards Writing Team. (2011, April 17). *Progressions for the Common Core State Standards in mathematics* [draft]. Available: commoncoretools.wordpress.com

Common Core State Standards Initiative. (2010a). *Application of Common Core State Standards for English language learners.* Washington, DC: CCSSO & National Governors Association. Retrieved from http://www.corestandards.org/assets/application-for-english-learners.pdf

Common Core State Standards Initiative. (2010b). *Application to students with disabilities.* Washington, DC: CCSSO & National Governors Association. Retrieved from http://www.corestandards.org/assets/application-to-students-with-disabilities.pdf

Common Core State Standards Initiative. (2010c). *Common Core State Standards for English language arts & literacy in history/social studies, science, and technical subjects.* Washington, DC: CCSSO & National Governors Association. Retrieved from http://www.corestandards.org/assets/CCSSI_ELA%20Standards.pdf

Common Core State Standards Initiative. (2010d). *Common Core State Standards for English language arts & literacy in history/social studies, science, and technical subjects. Appendix A: Research supporting key elements of the standards, glossary of key terms.* Washington, DC: CCSSO & National Governors Association. Retrieved from http://www.corestandards.org/assets/Appendix_A.pdf

Common Core State Standards Initiative. (2010e). *Common Core State Standards for English language arts & literacy in history/social studies, science, and technical subjects. Appendix B: Text exemplars and sample performance tasks.* Washington, DC: CCSSO & National Governors Association. Retrieved from http://www.corestandards.org/assets/Appendix_B.pdf

Common Core State Standards Initiative. (2010f). *Common Core State Standards for English language arts & literacy in history/social studies, science, and technical subjects. Appendix C: Samples of student writing.* Washington, DC: CCSSO & National Governors Association. Retrieved from http://www.corestandards.org/assets/Appendix_C.pdf

Common Core State Standards Initiative. (2010g). *Common Core State Standards for mathematics.* Washington, DC: CCSSO & National Governors Association. Retrieved from http://www.corestandards.org/assets/CCSSI_Math%20Standards.pdf

Dean, C. B., Hubbell, E. R., Pitler, H., & Stone, B. (2012). *Classroom instruction that works: Research-based strategies for increasing student achievement* (2nd ed.). Alexandria, VA: ASCD.

Fuys, D., Geddes, D., & Tischler, R. (1988). *The van Hiele model of thinking in geometry among adolescents. Journal for Research in Mathematics Education Monograph 3.* Reston, VA: NCTM.

Hess, K. (2011). *Learning progressions frameworks designed for use with the Common Core State Standards in English language arts & literacy K–12.* Retrieved from http://www.nciea.org/publication_PDFs/ELA_LPF_12%202011_final.pdf

Hess, K., & Hervey, S. (2011). *Tools for examining text complexity.* Retrieved from http://www.nciea.org/publication/

Kansas State Department of Education. (2011). *Text complexity resources.* Retrieved from http://www.ksde.org/Default.aspx?tabid=4778

Kendall, J. S. (2011). *Understanding Common Core State Standards.* Alexandria, VA: ASCD.

Kosanovich, M., & Verhagen, C. (2012). *Building the foundation: A suggested progression of sub-skills to achieve the reading standards: Foundational skills in the Common Core State Standards.* Portsmouth, NH: RMC Research Corporation, Center on Instruction.

Linder, S. M., Powers-Costello, B., & Stegelin, D. A. (2011, April). Mathematics in early childhood: Research-based rationale and practice strategies. *Early Childhood Education Journal, 39*(1), 29–37.

National Assessment Governing Board. (2010). *Reading framework for the 2011 National Assessment of Educational Progress*. Washington, DC: U.S. Government Printing Office Superintendent of Documents. Retrieved from http://www.nagb.org/publications/frameworks/reading-2011-framework.pdf

National Council of Teachers of Mathematics. (2000). *Principles and standards for school mathematics*. Reston, VA: Author.

National Institute of Child Health and Human Development. (2000). *Teaching children to read: An evidence-based assessment of the scientific research literature on reading and its implications for reading instruction: Report of the National Reading Panel*. (NIH Publication No. 00-4769). Washington, DC: U.S. Government Printing Office.

National Mathematics Advisory Panel. (2008). *Foundations for success: The final report of the National Mathematics Advisory Panel*. Washington, DC: U.S. Department of Education.

National Research Council. (2001). *Adding it up: Helping children learn mathematics*. Washington, DC: National Academies Press.

National Research Council, Committee on Early Childhood Mathematics. (2009). *Mathematics learning in early childhood: Paths towards excellence and equity*. Center for Education, Division of Behavioral and Social Sciences and Education. Washington, DC: National Academies Press.

Sarama, J., & Clements, D. H. (2009). *Early childhood mathematics education research: Learning trajectories for young children*. New York: Routledge.

Schmidt, W. (2012, May 3). *Common Core State Standards math: The relationship between high standards, systemic implementation and student achievement*. Paper presented at an event cosponsored by Achieve, Chiefs for Change, and the Foundation for Excellence in Education, Washington, D.C.

Shanahan, T. (2005). *The National Reading Panel report: Practical advice for teachers*. Naperville, IL: Learning Point Associates.

About the Authors

Amber Evenson is a lead consultant at Mid-continent Research for Education and Learning (McREL), providing services, strategies, and materials to support improvement in mathematics education, curriculum development, instructional coaching, and instructional technology. She also works with schools and districts to assist them as they align, plan, and implement the Common Core State Standards while building the internal capacity of the school or district. Ms. Evenson holds an MA in Teaching and Learning from Nova Southeastern University and a BA in Mathematics from Beloit College. Prior to coming to McREL, she served as a K–12 mathematics coach and has many years of experience as a secondary mathematics educator.

Monette McIver is a principal consultant at McREL and has worked on several design and development projects related to school leadership and systemic improvement efforts. A former assistant professor in the School of Education at the University of Colorado at Boulder, she taught a writing methods course for elementary teacher candidates and conducted research about writing instruction that focused on the interaction between teachers and students in the writing conference. Ms. McIver is an experienced elementary classroom teacher who has taught kindergarten through 4th grade. Her elementary classroom experiences include working with English language learners, adapting instruction to meet the diverse needs of learners, and mentoring preservice teachers. She is the coauthor of *Teaching Writing in the Content Areas.*

Susan Ryan is a senior consultant at McREL. She has reviewed, revised, and developed language arts standards documents for many districts, state agencies, and education organizations. Ms. Ryan has conducted alignment reviews on assessment items, instructional materials, and curriculum materials. Her work with the Common Core State Standards includes the production of gap analyses, crosswalks, transition documents, alignment reviews, and research support for state departments of education. Ms. Ryan has also facilitated teacher leaders in curriculum development and implementation of the Common Core. She was a consulting state content expert for English language arts during the development of the Common Core and a state consultant to the Partnership for Assessment of Readiness for College and Careers (PARCC) consortium. A former high school language arts teacher, she holds a BA in English from the University of Colorado and a secondary teaching license through Metropolitan State University of Denver.

 **Amitra Schwols** serves as a consultant at McREL. She has reviewed, revised, and developed standards documents for many districts, state agencies, and organizations. She has also reviewed instructional materials, created lesson plans, and conducted research on a wide variety of education topics. Ms. Schwols's work with the Common Core State Standards includes developing gap analysis, crosswalk, and transition documents, as well as facilitating implementation with groups of teacher leaders. She was a consulting state content expert for mathematics during the development of the Common Core standards and a state consultant to the Partnership for Assessment of Readiness for College and Careers (PARCC) consortium. A former classroom teacher at the secondary grades and a Navy veteran, Ms. Schwols holds a BS in Science with an emphasis in physics and mathematics and a minor in English from Colorado State University.

John Kendall (Series Editor) is Senior Director in Research at McREL in Denver. Having joined McREL in 1988, Mr. Kendall conducts research and development activities related to academic standards. He directs a technical assistance unit that provides standards-related services to schools, districts, states, and national and international organizations. He is the author of *Understanding Common Core State Standards,* the senior author of *Content Knowledge: A Compendium of Standards and Benchmarks for K–12 Education,* and the author or coauthor of numerous reports and guides related to standards-based systems. These works include *High School Standards and Expectations for College and the Workplace; Essential Knowledge: The Debate over What American Students Should Know;* and *Finding the Time to Learn: A Guide.* He holds an MA in Classics and a BA in English Language and Literature from the University of Colorado at Boulder.

About McREL

Mid-continent Research for Education and Learning (McREL) is a nationally recognized nonprofit education research and development organization headquartered in Denver, Colorado, with offices in Honolulu, Hawaii, and Omaha, Nebraska. Since 1966, McREL has helped translate research and professional wisdom about what works in education into practical guidance for educators. Our more than 120 staff members and affiliates include respected researchers, experienced consultants, and published writers who provide educators with research-based guidance, consultation, and professional development for improving student outcomes.

ASCD and Common Core State Standards Resources

ASCD believes that for the Common Core State Standards to have maximum effect, they need to be part of a well-rounded, whole child approach to education that ensures students are healthy, safe, engaged, supported, and challenged.

For a complete and updated overview of ASCD's resources related to the Common Core standards, including other *Quick-Start Guides* in the Understanding the Common Core Standards series, professional development institutes, online courses, links to webinars and to ASCD's free EduCore™ digital tool, and lots more, please visit us at **www.ascd.org/commoncore**.